DIFFERENT
WORLDS

DIFFERENT WORLDS

INTERRACIAL AND
CROSS-CULTURAL
DATING

BY JANET BODE

Franklin Watts
New York/London/Toronto/Sydney

Library of Congress Cataloging-in-Publication Data

Bode, Janet.
Different worlds : interracial and cross-cultural dating / by
Janet Bode.
p.   cm.
Bibliography: p.
Includes index.
Summary: Discusses the complex issues involved in interracial and
cross-cultural dating among teenagers, including parental reactions,
peer pressure, and psychological motivations.
ISBN 0-531-10663-2
1. Interracial dating—United States—Juvenile literature.
2. Interethnic dating—United States—Juvenile literature.
[1. Interracial dating. 2. Interethnic dating.] I. Title.
HQ801.8.B63 1989
306.7 3—dc19   88-30380 CIP AC

TO THE TEENAGERS

WHO SHARED THEIR STORIES

Also by Janet Bode

KIDS HAVING KIDS:

The Unwed Teenage Parent

CONTENTS

ACKNOWLEDGMENTS

It's hard to write a book. It's also exciting, brain-expanding, time-consuming, and fun. I thank my family and friends for always being there when I needed any or all of them during those difficult moments. Special praise goes to:

My father and fellow author, Carl Bode, and my stepmother, Charlotte, for advice and counsel.

My sisters, Barbara and Carolyn, for long-distance support.

My partner, Stan Mack, for editorial assistance and hand-holding.

My buddies near, Linda Broessel, Wendy Caplin, Andrea Eagan, Neil Hedin, Michael Kahan, Rosemarie and Marvin Mazor, Vince Pravata.

My buddies far, Lucy Cefalu, Carole Mayedo, Cindy Mitzel, Terry Thomas.

I received invaluable assistance from these other sources:

I.S. 88 (The Peter Rouget Intermediate School), Brooklyn, New York: student consultants—Akisa, Annette, Brenda, Evi, Genene, Gerard, Grace, Joanne, Josie, Hector, Marilu, Mayra, and Sandra; Steven Bram, their teacher; and Ginay Marks, Director, Alternative Drug Prevention Education Program, Community School Board District 15.

Project Reach, New York, New York: peer counselors—Kane, Sherine, Simon, and Wilson; student consultants—Daniel, Cho Hong, Henry, John, Norman, and Philip; Don Kao, Counselor/Director.

TO THE
READER

This book is based primarily on talks I had with teenagers across the country. Nearly all are dating someone whose race or background is different from their own. Some of the individuals come from wealthy homes and attend private schools. Others live in crowded, inner-city rental units and go to public schools. Still others live in the freeway-linked suburbs, or along the U.S.-Mexican border, or in the rolling countryside of farmlands dotted with occasional houses.

For an adult perspective, I also spoke to parents whose sons or daughters are involved in these relationships. And for further insight, I turned to a variety of experts: anthropologists, therapists, social historians, a medical doctor, teachers, and librarians. I interviewed, among others, Lynn Ponton, M.D., director, Adolescent Unit at Langley Porter Psychiatric Institute, University of California, and a child and adolescent psychiatrist; Mary Jo Nolin, Ph.D., sex educator on the high school level and sociologist with a specialty in social psychology and the sociology of the family; Polly Howells, C.S.W., a psycho-therapist with a private practice in Brooklyn, NY; and Ronny Diamond, M.S.W., C.S.W., faculty member at the Ackerman Institute for Family Therapy, and director of the Spence-Chapin Adoption Counseling Team, New York City.

The teen couples I talked to mentioned the sense of isolation they sometimes feel. They hoped that by sharing their experiences, others of you in similar situations would find emotional support and even some answers to difficult questions. They asked, however, that their privacy be protected. To do that, I changed their names and a few other details to conceal their identities. Their stories, though, remain accurate slices of real life.

DIFFERENT
WORLDS

1

RACIALLY-CULTURALLY-
ETHNICALLY SPEAKING

"So much for another summer romance," says seven-teen-year-old Jonathan, recalling his thoughts the day he flew home from his camp counselor job in Nevada. This strong-jawed, preppy type from Washington, D.C., admits to having had one or two "emotional flings" before. Serious flirting combined with promises followed by—zip, over and out—his description. But there he was, "grinning like a fool," holding hands with Heather at the airport as they prepared to go their separate ways. "Heather is this blond beauty with brains, and, boy, had I ever gotten attached to her during those seven weeks we'd worked together out West," says Jonathan. "I was trying to be Mr. Cool, but the words coming from my mouth didn't sound anything like 'good-bye.' Instead, this voice—my voice, imagine—was announcing, 'I'm going to take you to my school prom.'"

Heather, a Philadelphia resident, says with a peaches-and-cream blush, "When he said that about his prom, I began to answer, 'Great, and I'll take you to my . . .' And then I stopped, realizing I can't take him to my senior prom. What am I doing? A zillion things were running through my head. I was upset and just about crying, mentally debating, Why am I sad that I'm going to leave him? I have the semiperfect boyfriend waiting for me. Jonathan is wonderful, but he lives two hours away by train. Why would I want to complicate my life with him, especially when none of my friends is dating someone who's different? It was fun while it lasted. I had the best time with him, though, and I care for him a lot. Why does he have to be *black*!''

At Washington's Dulles Airport, Heather left to make her connecting flight home, while Jonathan and his mother went in search of his baggage. Twelve days would pass before the next move was made. Who called whom first? That issue remains open for debate. Heather remembers Jonathan phoning, but he insists it was the other way around. What they do agree on is that that call set the stage for a new phase of their relationship. Their feelings for each other grew in direct proportion to the size of their phone bills. By call three, they admitted that they really wanted to get together as soon as possible, which turned out to be the following week. Jonathan discovered an uncle in Philadelphia he just had to visit.

There was a rain cloud of reality, though, hovering over their excitement. In the descriptions of their summer adventures they'd offered to friends and family, Heather (but not Jonathan) had omitted what some might consider a critical detail. ''I left out that we're different races; that he's black,'' Heather says of this five-foot-ten-inch charmer. ''What I was more likely to mention were his good looks and his wacky sense of humor.''

CAST OF CHARACTERS

Jonathan and Heather are just one of the couples you'll meet on these pages. They both come from middle-class homes and attend urban private schools. You'll also read about Theresa and Scott who live in rural America, close to the U.S.-Mexican border. "We're from a little bitty Rio Grande Valley [Texas] town, population twenty thousand. It's got lots more farms and ranches than grocery stores," says Theresa, a sixteen-year-old junior and pep club member who traces her roots to Mexico and Spain. Decades ago, her boyfriend's family immigrated here from Scotland. "In this neck of the woods, the mixture of the two of us together can sure spell trouble," Theresa adds, with the look of a person who's been through some.

On the West Coast, there's Kenny and Mina, residents of one of the freeway-linked sections of the megalopolis, Los Angeles. As with the others, these fifteen-year-old sophomores are caught in a racial and cultural crossfire. He's labeled white while she's Asian—Chinese-American to be exact. Explains Kenny, "My supposedly liberal mom is freaked out by our relationship, and, according to Mina's mother and father, she's not even allowed to date."

In the eight months that a couple named Irene and Ruben have been seeing each other, she's gone through a series of parental warnings to stop the relationship. She's been hounded and grounded and has seen her phone privileges vanish. Once she was told she'd be sent to live with relatives if she didn't mend her ways. The problem? These Cincinnati, Ohio, seniors may share interests, but not their cultural heritage. Although they are both American-born, Irene's family is Indian, by way of South Africa, while Ruben's mother is Puerto Rican and his father, Cuban.

You'll read about Sara, who's white, and Benigno, nicknamed Bennie, who's Filipino. The relationship between this Staten Island, New York, twosome wasn't met with quite universal approval. Nor was that of Kelly and Randall, a white and black duo from Dunwoody, Georgia, outside Atlanta. They could only see each other at school.

These teenagers—and maybe you, too—are learning one of life's lessons. Many in this nation are convinced that it's wrong to date someone of a different race or someone whose background is not the same as your own. At the least, you are walking a tricky line. In *theory* and *law*, here in the United States, all people—race or ethnic origin aside—are considered equals. The color of your skin or the country from which your family originally comes doesn't matter. All people can live as neighbors, attend the same school, worship together, marry, and even have kids. In *reality* and *practice*, however, no matter how Jonathan and Heather or the others may view one another, society sees them through the distorted lens of a troubled racial and cultural history.

THE INVENTION OF RACE

Anthropology professor and author of the book *The Origin and Evolution of the Idea of Race*, Audrey Smedley, Ph.D. says that "it was only about three or four hundred years ago that a new kind of race awareness was invented. Before that, different populations recognized their diversity and interacted with one another. But they didn't establish any ordering system of racial classifications. That had never been done before."

For the first time, European experts of the day more or less officially decided that yes, they, themselves, were fair-skinned and round-eyed. And yes, there were the broad-lipped, darker-skinned peoples of Africa; and the peoples of Asia, most of whom had light brown complexions, straight hair, and a skin fold over the eye. What they didn't know was that many of these external differences represent minor evolutionary changes. Skin color, for instance, is only an adaptation to climate—white in Europe to absorb ultraviolet radiation that helps make vitamin D, black in Africa for protection from the sun. Instead, they simply took what they saw, and from that limited view, using a number of physical characteristics, they cut up the world populations into three major pieces: Caucasoid, loosely defined as "white"; Negroid, loosely defined as "black"; and Mongoloid, loosely defined as "yellow."

Their next intertwined steps were far grimmer. After arbitrarily separating people into races, the experts made a giant leap. They concluded that some races were born smarter or more talented or with a better way of life. They attributed this to differences in physical appearance. How members of a certain race behaved was fused with how they looked. This, in turn, opened the final door. People made moral judgments on each race's worth.

Different populations could be ranked superior or inferior, good or bad. Those doing the ranking—the Europeans who at that moment in history were into exploring and colonizing world wide—decided that they themselves were a chosen people with a divine ordination from God. They ignored the fact that centuries earlier inhabitants of parts of Africa and the Middle East had civilizations far more advanced than theirs. They simply pressed on, deciding that the other races were, in many ways, savages.

Savages, this theory went, were not fully human. They were shifty, barbaric. They lacked intellectual ability. They were incapable of being civilized. And because they were fundamentally different from Europeans, it was all right to treat them in whatever way the Europeans pleased. They treated them brutally or benevolently, but always from a superior point of view.

"All this led into racism—that form of prejudice where you believe that other races are inferior to yours; and by the eighteenth century, race had become part of our social consciousness. It also had become one of the major factors in defining a person's social identity," says Dr. Smedley, adding that even into the 1930s and 1940s, scientists were basing conclusions about what was going on in the brains of the different races by measuring skulls. "Still today, this fusion of what seemed to be inherited physical characteristics with moral worth has persisted in being the unspoken element in the idea of race."

Another anthropologist, a professor at New York University, explains that eventually, as scientists and scientific methods grew more sophisticated, they realized that the concept of racial grouping was more complicated than simple division into three separate parts. The world populations just didn't fit. Rather, they began to cite nine—and sometimes ten—racial groups: African, American Indian, Asian, Australian, European, Indian, Melanesian, Micronesian, and Polynesian. And while physical characteristics continued to be the means of differentiating one race from the others, blood type started to be included as an important determining factor, too.

"Scientists tried isolating certain populations, certain groups of people, where they found more of one characteristic than another," says the professor. "But in the end—although blood type helps us find out about such things as resistance to various diseases—the shape of one's lips or the presence or absence of skin folds above the eye simply isn't important. Those traits are distributed across an entire population. There's a great deal of variation within the races and a great deal of overlap among them, as well. In other words, say you take the color of skin for members of one race. There is a distribution going from very light all the way to very dark, and this is true not only for those called blacks. With so much mixture, the problem lies in where to define the boundaries of what a race is. Today race is looked at as a social concept more than a scientific one."

A COMMON CULTURE

There's another vital ingredient attached to society's view of race. It's called culture. Many people confuse race and culture. Today, America is home to more nationalities than ever before. You'll find Samoans, Egyptians, and Japanese; Panamanians, Jordanians, and Lebanese. Regardless of whether any individual member of a group has lived within these borders a month or a lifetime, to varying degrees you will still share with your own people what is known as a common culture, a common ethnic background. You have the same customs, language, and attitudes. To varying degrees, members of your group, your nationality, live in both worlds—that of your original homeland and that of this country, the past and the future.

What this means is the following. Racial divisions and moral judgments go together with cultural ones. They're related, part of the same "family" of problems. The words "Stick to your own kind" often translate to "Only date people of your nationality," as well as of the same race. When an interracial or cross-cultural couple first meet, consciously or unconsciously you see each other mirrored in your family's and the nation's eyes. You don't need anyone to point out that you come with two different racial or ethnic labels. And you sense—you know—that with mixed dating, although you might be looking at love, you are also looking at trouble.

JONATHAN AND HEATHER

Jonathan and Heather's story started last spring, bringing with it both storms and flowers. Before they even discovered that the other existed, they both happened to sign up with the same special camp program as counselors for inner-city kids in a rugged Nevada setting. "The end of June when we all arrived, naturally, everyone immediately checks out the opposite sex: five guys to eight sort of ho-hum girls," says Jonathan, describing his first reaction to Heather. "I remember thinking, This is going to be a long summer."

Heather recalls that their meeting began when she and another counselor were busy with their own evaluation. "We decided that one of the guys was a short goof, one a tall goof, one a scrawny Kansan who might be cool but no one you'd want to date, one possible, and then there was Jonathan. I didn't realize until later, halfway through the program when we were talking about our first impressions of each other, that I didn't even *have* a first impression. I'd totally skipped over him when I saw the guys. At that moment, when I thought about who I might go out with, I didn't consider him. He was not even in my range of options."

As the weeks went by, all the teen counselors grew to be close friends. During the day, they were absorbed in trying to help the campers acquire new skills, from riding horses to building cookout fires to scaling mountainsides. But at night and in their free time, they'd hang out in the main cabin and talk. It was during these random hours that Jonathan and Heather began to exchange life histories.

They talked about their advanced placement (A.P.) classes and their classmates. While the student body at Jonathan's school is racially mixed, there are no minorities in Heather's senior class. "In the junior class, there's only one, although the lower grades have a few because they were actively recruited." They talked about their current interests. Jonathan's active in Minorities Against Discrimination, M.A.D., where, among other projects, the members raise money for the homeless and tutor elementary school minority students. "It's important for these kids to have role models," he had explained to Heather, who admits that before their conversations her idea of an important concern was what to wear the next day. ("I'm not an airhead," she says. "I was simply focused on my own priorities"—the school play, the girls' soccer team, drum lessons, and the job of features editor of the yearbook.)

"Oh, by the way," began the sentence in which Heather tried casually at camp to lob this emotional time bomb, "I do have a boyfriend, Max, back home." As the sun eased below the horizon, the sky turned into a prism of colors. It was week three of the seven-week program, and by then the two of them were beginning to spend time just with each other. "Dump him," Jonathan jokingly responded. They laughed. Although they knew they were strongly attracted to one another, they also categorized their emotions as a summer romance. ("But maybe with capital letters," says Heather.) They agreed, their budding romance was carefree and great—for Nevada, hundreds of miles away from their real friends and their real worlds. Anyway, both of them had gone away for summers before and that's what happens.

"Back at school, I'd always be the one with the cute boyfriend, the one with the summer romance with the gorgeous, blond lifeguard. I'd show my girlfriends his picture saying, 'Look at him; isn't he beautiful?' Sure, Jonathan's really handsome, but somehow, right then when I tried to imagine myself showing his photo to my friends—all of them are white—he couldn't be considered good-looking, because he was black. And I sure didn't know how they'd handle that fact, either."

By the time the program reached week five, Jonathan heard himself telling Heather, then telling her again, that he loved her. He didn't want her to see any other guys when she returned to Philadelphia. "I'd had boyfriends since I was in the third grade," recalls Heather. "I had my first real go-to-the-movies date in eighth grade. In all that time, I'd never told any of them that I loved him. For me, Jonathan was still a summer interruption to my serious high school relationship. Max and I had been dating for a long time, two months. He goes to my rival school where he's the ultimate jock, the captain of the football team. He's also the most fabulous-looking thing you've ever seen, and has his own car. It was fun when he'd pick me up at my school. But to put it bluntly, I admit, Max is kind of a jerk."

And then week seven. The plane ride brought Jonathan and Heather back to reality, back to fall classes.

LEARNING THE RULES

Although Jonathan and Heather—and you, as well— might not be able to define or categorize race or cultural divisions from any scientific point of view, from early childhood everyone starts to pick up bits and pieces of what anthropologists call social definitions. Even infants distinguish between the familiar and the strange. By the age of three, most of you could categorize your own gender. Within the next couple of years, you could correctly categorize others.

Around the age of four or five, you also start to learn a few more details about who you are, about your ethnic background, and how you fit into society's framework. Writes Howard J. Ehrlich in his book *The Social Psychology of Prejudice*, young children "begin developing ethnic attitudes even before developing the ability to correctly identify those to whom [those attitudes] are directed. . . ."[1] And parents teach this information "in much the same way they instruct the child in all other modes of proper behavior." You learn about race and ethnic diversity at your parent's knee. You learn which population groups have the power, and which don't. You learn in a general way what the different groups physically look like, and how to tell them apart.

From a young age, everyone absorbs these lessons and interprets the cues of what roles society casts for you and for others. By now, you intuitively know how your part of the world perceives the differences among the races and ethnic groups. If you saw Jonathan and Heather, you'd know who's called black and who's called white. You also know that in terms of this country's population, there is a white majority and a black minority. You know that much of the wealth and the heaviest concentration of power are held in white hands.

In Heather's case, she knows that she lives in an all-white, urban-suburban neighborhood. If she notices any blacks on those streets, they are as likely as not in service positions. Jonathan, who lives in the somewhat racially mixed urban area of Washington's Capitol Hill, knows that while he wasn't even born when local black residents rioted—because of Martin Luther King, Jr.'s assassination and unfulfilled promises of more jobs and better living conditions—the resulting empty shells of buildings that he passes on his way to school have never been completely rebuilt or replaced. White and black priorities frequently fail to converge.

Jonathan and Heather, along with the rest of you, learn your own family's feeling about yourselves and the people with whom you share a common ethnic background or culture. You learn your family's thoughts about people whom you think of as "others." And if asked, both Jonathan and Heather could tell you what their families value. Jonathan might mention the emphasis his family places on getting a solid education. Heather, who is Irish Catholic, might discuss the significance of religion in her daily life.

A dictionary definition of race reads like this: any of the major biological divisions of mankind, distinguished by color and texture of hair, color of skin and eyes, stature, bodily proportions. A family, tribe, people, or nation belonging to the same stock. Its social definition—the words you use—is not as straightforward or simple. Separating ethnic groups and labels can be just as confusing, too. What any of the terms mean to you and what labels you apply to a particular group or individual member is as much a matter of your family's economic class—how rich or how poor your are—as your age, your educational level, your cultural heritage, and your own world view. Or it can just depend on the era and the part of the country where you happen to live at the time.

LABELS

Talk to Jonathan and he'll explain that when his father was being raised in Alabama forty-odd years ago, whites usually referred to his dad as "colored," while he himself used the word "Negro." During the late 1960s, the word "black" began to be his choice and continues to be what he considers appropriate today. On occasion, however, he's been known to use the label "Afro-American."

Jonathan's mother is white. Because of that, Jonathan defines himself as biracial, a member of two races. However, since labels are based on externals, on what society sees, society calls him black. When he dates someone who's white, society insists that with the two of them together, the label interracial must be applied.

The other couples in this book agree that labeling is no exact science. More to the point, it can be silly. But what labels you do use speak volumes about how you feel about a particular group of people. Theresa explains that in Texas and much of the Southwest, because of her Mexican-Spanish heritage, she's usually labeled Mexican, Mexican-American, or Spanish. "People call me Spanish when they're trying to flatter me," says Theresa with a smile. "I've got fair skin, light brown hair, and was born in this country. You'd think by the labels I was some kind of outsider, not a real American."

In that part of the country, her boyfriend, Scott, with just the same coloring and place of birth, is referred to as Anglo, derived from the term Anglo-Saxon. His ancestors two generations back came from Scotland. If Theresa had any New York City cousins, they would probably call themselves American, Hispanic, or Latino. On the West Coast, people with Theresa's same ethnic background sometimes prefer the word Chicano.

Mina, now a naturalized U.S. citizen, was born in mainland China. When asked how she'd respond to the question, "What nationality or race are you?" she says that over the last few years she has said she's American, Chinese, Chinese-American, Asian, and Asian-American. She feels the racial designation "Mongolian" is outdated, the descriptive term "yellow," insulting. Her boyfriend, Kenny, along with a quarter of this country's population, claims some German heritage. "I like German food, bratwurst and sauerkraut," says Kenny. "But I think of myself as American. And when I'm filling out a form, I check the box that is marked 'white' or 'Caucasian.'"

Because Irene looks quite exotic with her dusky complexion, oval eyes, and wavy dark hair, people are often curious or perplexed about her heritage. Her answer, she says, depends on her mood; American, Indian, Asian-Indian, or South African are her replies. Says Irene, "Those last two answers in particular stop them. Sitars and apartheid? They don't know what to think, or I get just blank stares. They know so little about either land."

Her boyfriend, Ruben, on the other hand, sometimes is taken for black. He says that before his parents' and grandparents' generation in Puerto Rico and Cuba, who knows what happened in his relatives' lives. He guesses that some African genes are mixed in with the rest, remnants of the slave trade from centuries gone by. Although he feels multiracial and multicultural, he usually prefers the label Latino.

People such as Ruben, Irene, Theresa, and Jonathan are getting harder to label. You're not talking just about race; you're also talking about culture or ethnic background. These teenagers understand, maybe better than many people, that appearances are frequently deceptive and labeling creates traps. Throughout this book, these two issues of interracial and cross-cultural dating will often be linked and treated as one.

2

PREJUDICE—OR ALL DOMINICANS DANCE THE MERENGUE

Interracial or cross-cultural dating doesn't enter your life alone. Stealthily, menacingly, prejudice too often follows close on its heels.

What causes prejudice in society in the first place, and what keeps it holding on? Put simply, experts say, all of you believe the way *you* look and act is normal and right and, therefore, desirable. Those who disagree with you, who hold different views are, well, "different," "outsiders." You distrust them, those "others" who look and act strange. And the more obvious the differences, the greater the alarm. You may feel suspicion, intolerance, and even hate, emotions that can escalate into a we-versus-they concept of life. Then, directly and indirectly, year by year, these same lessons are passed from one generation to the next.

Psychotherapist Polly Howells, C.S.W., who has a private practice in Brooklyn, New York, where she sees individual teenagers and adults, as well as entire families, explains it this way: "Many people need to feel special, because inside they don't feel very secure. How they get that kind of specialness, that sense of security, is by banding together into a group. Whether they do it openly or in a more secret manner, the message remains clear— they're better than other people. They have to guard their boundaries against outsiders. If the 'others' get in, they will contaminate the group. If they can stay united, they will be out of danger and maintain their unique and pure form."

BREAKING THE RULES

Almost twenty years ago, Jonathan's mother endured the results of breaking society's "rules" on who's right to date and who's not. When she started dating the man who became Jonathan's father, her parents insisted they stop seeing each other. She was making a tragic error, her parents said. The relationship would fail; her life would be ruined. She shouldn't ever consider marrying him. "Your own kind, that's best," they told her. "What about Mrs. Shelby's son? He's such a nice fellow." But Jonathan's mother was young and headstrong and in love. She ignored their words of warning. The problem, they reminded her in exasperation, was that she was white and he wasn't. He was black. While she believed that was unimportant, most of the world didn't agree. "Look at the individual, the man, not at your preconceptions and misconceptions of his race," she would counter.

Within three years, they became husband and wife, Jonathan was born, and the marriage ended. (But not for the reasons her parents predicted, Jonathan's mother later revealed to her son. What put a division between them was not their races, not the different colors of their skin. It was because the two of them had been raised in very different types of homes; they had different value systems, different educational levels, different notions of how to spend money and how to use time.)

Jonathan's grandparents, however, cut their daughter out of their lives and only gradually did they allow her to return to the family. They didn't meet Jonathan, their grandson, until his sixth birthday. Those tough years filled with loneliness and despair ended on a note of triumph. Today, Jonathan has his grandparents' blood, their love and their joy. And his mother is a respected, happily remarried lawyer.

Heather's background is a variation on that same theme: what can happen when you cross cultural lines. When her mother was seventeen, she fell in love with someone who had a different ethnic background. Her strongly Irish-Catholic parents were furious their child was involved with a person they referred to as "that Englishman."

It didn't matter, they said, that he had been born and raised in the United States. It didn't matter that so had his parents. He was English. How did Heather's mother meet her parents' concerns about their daughter's future and further education? She ran away from home.

She didn't want to hear about their feelings on the English. They weren't, in her opinion, all bloodthirsty Protestants who should leave the Irish alone. (But in the heart and mind of her father, especially, remained a bitter rage fueled by the centuries old hostility between these two nations. His father and his father's father before that had hated the English. He would be no different. "What a horrible family tradition," was his daughter's response, before suggesting he "give up his anger.")

Within a few months, when Heather's mother became pregnant by this man with English roots, he responded that at age nineteen he was too young to be a father. The mother-to-be vowed to "show them all" as she went on to raise the child on her own.

Heather has vivid memories of her unique early years—hitchhiking and living on communes with her mother in this country and in Europe. There's nothing much she wants to say about her biological father. She never knew him, and her mother tells her he was certainly no help to either her or their daughter.

Now almost two decades later, in this situation Heather's mother has beaten the odds. In fact, she's flourished. Her recent marriage to a man who happens to have her parents' approval is as successful as her professional life. She's a financial analyst for a large bank. Heather, however, knows that although she loves her mother's parents—and they very much love her—there is one group of people they hate as much as the English. Her grandfather doesn't have a single good thing to say about blacks.

AS AMERICAN
AS APPLE PIE

Some people say that prejudice—at least the particular brand aimed at a specific race or culture—is as American as apple pie. It's been around since unknown numbers of the original residents, the Native Americans, were slaughtered by the European-born settlers in their sweep westward across the land. Blacks, at various times in our checkered history, have been denied the basic right to eat in a local diner or to drink from the closest water fountain. As a people, they've been victims of slavery, lynching, rape, and murder.

When Irish immigrants of the mid-nineteenth century arrived on these shores looking for work, they found that the American welcome mat came with strings attached. Signs greeted them, stating they "need not apply" for the jobs they wanted so badly. Italians who came here after the Civil War were met with the same open scorn and derision. Catholics were feared; Quakers persecuted. Jews were both barred and had quotas maintained against them. During World War II, whole Japanese-American families were forced from their homes and interned in the equivalent of prisons. Today, the most recent immigrants from Asian, Caribbean, African, and Latin-American countries have experienced their own sad share of discrimination and blatant prejudice.

Only about one and a half million residents of the United States can claim descent from the original inhabitants, the Native Americans. For the rest of the 245 million, each family tree includes an immigrant—by choice or by force—from some other part of the globe. Throughout these years of immigration, the idea of America as a place where different cultures and backgrounds blended into one became a vivid part of our national image. Jean de Crèvecoeur, a French nobleman and later a gentleman farmer and naturalized U.S. citizen, is credited with being the first person to describe this country as a melting pot. The year was 1782.

"The melting pot theory was okay," says Jesse Lemisch, Ph.D., an American studies and history professor at the State University of New York, Buffalo, "but it had a bad underside. It was a way to get rid of differing cultures and to erase ethnic pride. In other words, it was a way to escape from dealing with the reality of prejudice."

Of course, prejudice is far from unique to this country. It's been part of world history since time began. Two thousand years ago the Greeks and the Romans enslaved those people they considered inferior. For hundreds of years following Marco Polo's journey to the Orient in A.D. 1200, the Chinese referred to Westerners as "hairy white barbarians." The anger, distrust, and fury between Israelis and Arabs in the Middle East, blacks and Afrikaners in South Africa, to name four different groups, can be read about in newspapers daily.

PREJUDGING

Prejudice in its most concise form means prejudging. It means holding an opinion without just grounds or sufficient knowledge, believing that something is cold, hard fact without bothering to make any verification. It's the I-hate-rutabagas approach, when you've never even seen one. But as you know, prejudice can and does take a human toll; victim and victimizer, getting and giving, in a relentless, eternal cycle. All of society pays the price and is the poorer for it.

Jonathan says that the other day when he and a bunch of white buddies piled into a deli for a snack after a ball game, he was the one whom the owner kept eyeing with suspicion. "Because of my skin color, he automatically treated me like some kind of villain."

Mina was confused when she first came to this country. Before, she'd been "just another Chinese." Now, overnight, she was different, a minority. "Shortly after we arrived, I was walking in my Los Angeles neighborhood with my parents and cousin when we passed a group of white teenagers. One of them yelled, 'Look out for the Chink invasion.' My father told us, 'Don't stoop to their level. Keep walking.' I could hear those guys laughing and saying, 'See, they *are* all quiet.' I thought, 'If this is how Chinese are treated, I don't want to be Chinese.'"

When Ruben was about seven, some kids started pushing him around. "Then I was too young to understand they did it because I'm Latino. I started to cry. I wasn't ready to fight. Not until I was ten did I know the reasons behind their actions. Once when a landlord wouldn't rent to my parents, we could tell it was because he was prejudiced. They fought it legally. They could *do* something. But what do I do when I'm insulted because of the way I talk or the color of my skin? I try to ignore it, but sometimes I want to get them back. Answer them, and I'm playing their game. They're in control. What I hate about prejudice is it makes me feel so bad inside."

CULTURAL CHARACTERISTICS

Prejudice is an attitude of hostility directed against an individual, a group, a race, or the race's supposed social or cultural characteristics. The word to watch here is "characteristics." Researchers have discovered that even among those of you who don't consider yourself prejudiced, you still see groups of people in terms of certain characteristics, everything from how smart you perceive them to be to their lack of skill driving a car.

What you might consider a compliment, such as saying, "All Chinese are great at kung fu," or "All Dominicans dance a hot merengue," is still categorizing groups of people. That's not so far removed from "All Colombians deal drugs" or "All Iranians are religious fanatics." Those characteristics, good or bad, combine to make up what's called a racial or cultural stereotype.

Randall, the senior from Georgia, complains that he's tired of being stereotyped. He's tired of hearing "All blacks have rhythm"; "all blacks are lazy." But the one that gets him the most is, "All blacks are born athletes." He says, "I practice, man, practice. I work at my dribbling, my lay-ups, my foul shots. I'm at it until the sun goes down and I can't see anymore. When I hear, 'Oh, it's inborn,' that takes away from the credit I feel I have earned."

Randall isn't alone. For each race, each nationality, there are a series of stereotypes. The Irish are drunkards, romantics, and full of blarney. Puerto Ricans are noisy. Hondurans talk too fast. Samoans are fat. Theresa with her Mexican-Spanish heritage says the attitude she hears from some Anglos is, "All Mexican guys are dope smokers with switchblades and all Mexican girls fool around. Mention Mexicans and half the world comes up with the picture of someone with a sombrero on his head sleeping under a tree. With that attitude, I start out my life in an uphill battle against those faulty images."

HOW PREJUDICE
GAINS A FOOTHOLD

There is a deeply rooted tendency to perceive, to categorize, and to label people according to the group to which they belong. The group label then takes on a particular power. The individual is seen in terms of the group label, the group stereotype, instead of in terms of his or her own particular personality.

"Your ability to categorize people is one of the things that makes life go smoothly," says Mary Jo Nolin, Ph.D., a Washington, D.C., sex educator and sociologist who specializes in social psychology and the sociology of the family. The world around you is chaotic, so filled with people and things and places that the mind looks for ways to simplify this enormous amount of data. One of the ways to start organizing it is to lump people into groups.

"Let's say you go to the department store," says Dr. Nolin. "Once there, you don't have to wonder what to say to the salesclerks. You are there to purchase; they are there to aid. You don't need to know whether they have a happy life or what they had for breakfast. You don't need to deal with those issues in order to buy what you want. Because you've categorized those people, you know how to behave in that particular interaction.

"You carry that a step further and you learn that when you see people for the first time, you relate to them on the basis of their sex—whether they're male or female—then visual clues as to their age, their race, and their culture. In other words, when you come to an encounter with a stranger, you already have certain expectations that give you a structure in which to deal with each other. And that works fine in those situations where all you need know is the person's role. But problems begin when you *only* see the stereotype, and never notice the person."

You don't see Bennie for himself; you may not have the time. And you may not have the interest. Instead, you see him as a Filipino. Whatever conclusions you've come to about people from that country, you wrap around Bennie. You don't see Jonathan or Randall. You don't see Sara or Heather. You don't see Theresa, Mina, or Ruben. You see instead two blacks, two whites, a Mexican-American, a Chinese, and a Latino.

Real social interaction requires going beyond the initial, simple categorizing. It means exploring one another's lives and ideas, learning about the individual behind the group label. If you stop doing that—or worse, have never done it—this natural process of stereotyping and categorizing people turns sour. By becoming a distortion of the process that helps you order and organize your world, it brings on the destructive side of prejudice.

In addition, because you tend to be selective in what you remember, over the years the stereotypes and categories you develop serve to confirm what you've let yourself believe. Those who are highly prejudiced will often tell others about "bad" experiences with persons who are members of some other race or ethnic group. "Once you've decided, for instance, that all Koreans are passive and conservative, it's hard to change your mind. You look for and remember events that reinforce your beliefs, while avoiding those that do not," says Dr. Nolin. "Even if I introduced you to this wonderful, lively, hysterically funny Korean person you'd probably tell me, 'Oh, he's the exception. All other Koreans are reserved.'"

So what does all this mean to the interracial or the cross-cultural couple?

For better or worse, the potential of prejudice—in you as well as in others—turns you and your partner into a trio. This unwelcome, crippling force is, by definition, your companion. Prejudice can strike anytime, anywhere, and without warning. As a result, one of your most important tasks becomes answering these questions: Can I handle the pressure? And is the relationship worth it?

3

GUESS WHO'S COMING
TO DINNER?

How do parents react when they learn their son or daughter is dating someone whose background isn't a reflection of their own? The range of reaction is enormous. There's Jonathan and Heather's situation where both sets of parents are supportive; and there's Theresa and Scott where her parents are fine, but his mother has actually threatened physical violence. Somewhere along this continuum are Kenny and Mina. His mother is subtly disapproving, and her parents technically don't even allow her to date.

In Jonathan's case, his mother tried to prepare him for the possibility of interracial dating ahead of time. Jonathan reports that she'd say, "Some day you may go out with a white girl; and sometimes her family or friends might not approve. You have to be ready for that." He'd tell her, "Nope, not me. That's not going to happen." Until it did. He hasn't received any more recent advice because, in his opinion, his mother really doesn't take this relationship with Heather very seriously. And right now, that's okay, since he doesn't want to offer her any more personal details.

Heather says her "mother and stepfather love Jonathan." In fact, it was easier to tell them about her new boyfriend than to confide in her best friend. After spending a weekend with Heather's parents and a couple of aunts and uncles, Jonathan received high marks. "Although my relationship with my mother isn't always a whole pile of monkeys, we get along pretty well. When we have disagreements, they're serious, but none has been about Jonathan. She treats him like any other boyfriend, except she reminds me—as if she had to—not to mention anything about him to my grandfather."

While other teenagers may have parental problems on this issue, Heather's grandfather and his racist attitudes have been the cause of some of her and Jonathan's heaviest fights. Because her grandparents' home is within blocks of hers, they're a strong presence in her life. Since she first started dating, it's been a tradition for her to bring around boyfriends for their approval. Once, when the boyfriend wasn't Catholic, her grandfather was displeased. Heather didn't want to conjure up any mental images of how a meeting between Jonathan and him might go.

"The man is totally, outwardly racist," says Jonathan, adding that he could not not take it personally. "I remind myself it doesn't have anything to do with me, the individual. That keeps me from getting angry for a max of three minutes. The bottom line is that Heather can't tell him she's going out with me because that would ruin *their* relationship. Well, what about *our* relationship?"

Heather acknowledges, "My grandfather has no shame about saying horrible things about black people. But he's almost eighty, stubborn to boot, and doesn't know any other way of thinking. Jonathan believes that if I tell my grandfather about us, he'll change his racist views. I see where Jonathan's coming from and that's a nice idea, but it's not going to work."

You can feel Jonathan switch from frustration to anger and back again. "If everyone thought that way, no one's opinion would ever be changed. You'd never speak out against anything. What if Martin Luther King, Jr. had said that there's no use in trying to change America? You've just got to do it whether the person you're confronting is old or young," Jonathan says, before agreeing to yet another truce on this issue.

KENNY AND MINA

Kenny and Mina, the Los Angeles couple, might wish they only had a grandfather to contend with. They're caught in the middle of three parents prejudiced in their own particular way. This relationship started one afternoon in biology class when Kenny and Mina were assigned to dissect the same frog. They were much more interested in each other.

"Our school has a student body of about twelve hundred students, sixty percent white, forty percent Asian, mainly Chinese-American, that is," says Kenny, who's white and a self-described "good-time" sophomore. "I like to have fun and get along with most everyone. I've had every color friend you can imagine." His family moved to L.A. from Colorado when he was around four and soon settled in a section reported to have an excellent school system. What they hadn't planned on was "this influx of Chinese," as his mother puts it. She feels comfortable around blacks and Chicanos, Kenny heard her telling a neighbor, but these last few years, she's "overwhelmed by the Chinese."

Now at age fifteen, Kenny's a member of a blended family. "My parents are divorced, and I live with my mom. But at Christmas and during the summer I stay with my dad, my stepmother, and her two kids in Santa Monica, close to the pier."

His parents are "liberals," he says, explaining he still recalls being taught to "recycle tin cans, use only biodegradable paper products, and understand the necessity of zero population growth." Considering his upbringing, what surprised him was his mother's not-always-subtle pressure to stop seeing Mina. "It all started when she learned that my first serious girlfriend happened to be Asian," says Kenny.

His mother's attitude now seems to be, he believes, that it is all right to be friends with people from different races and cultures, but not to date. Mina's parents are even stricter. They emigrated from China a decade earlier and carried with them their beliefs on how to raise children. At fifteen, they believe Mina is too young to date. Kenny and Mina are ignoring their parents.

Mina rationalizes her relationship with Kenny by convincing herself that they aren't actually dating. Yes, they sit next to each other in biology class; and yes, they've been known to go over to his house after school for an hour or two before his mother gets home from work. "But so what?" says Mina. "We don't really go out—out, like to the movies or to parties. And Kenny knows that he shouldn't call me. I'm not allowed to talk on the phone except for a total of a half hour, anyway."

Mina's mother instructs her that she must keep her mind on education and stay away from "boys, especially seedy, gangster types." "Even if I brought home an Asian guy, my mother would be hysterical. She'd immediately think I was getting married. I can't ever date anyone Japanese. Nanjing, China, my mother's family's home, was invaded by Japan and thousands of people were raped and slaughtered. My mother has lots of hatred toward them as a result. Many older Chinese people do. Eventually, maybe a Korean-American or someone from

Thailand would be okay for me to date; I don't know for sure."

What would happen if she invited Kenny over to introduce him to her parents? "Forget it. I'd hear a lot of negative attitudes. 'You're turning your back on our culture. You'll forget who you are and everything we value highly. He comes from an alien world. He's unsuitable. He's a threat.' And, even though my mother—she's the disciplinarian—doesn't speak very much English, she knows how to say, 'No, you can't.' My mother and father would deny they are prejudiced. They would probably explain that they are simply preserving our heritage."

Recently, to see if her parents might have softened their views, Mina brought home a new girlfriend. She came to this country several years ago from Malaysia. This friend not only could date, she could date anyone she wanted. In front of her mother, Mina asked her friend, "Why don't you have any dating restrictions?" She answered, "My country is multiracial, a festival of people. My parents are used to mixing." "Festival, phooey," Mina's mother said in Chinese. She was not impressed. She did not like her daughter's new friend.

"I remind myself, as a family, we went through a lot to move here," says Mina, who lives in a rambling four-bedroom home with her parents, her grandmother, and a cousin. "My father works very hard and does well. Still, in China, the children are expected to do better than the parents. And you are supposed to obey your parents. I don't really like being up to things that I know would anger them.

"But, at the same time, inside, I feel American. I love hanging out at Two-Heys, a local hamburger place. I love shopping at the Santa Anita Mall. About two years ago, I didn't feel like I wanted to be Asian. I'd say, 'I'm not Asian. I'm American.' Today, I appreciate being Asian. I got very angry when I discovered that once there was a law in this town that said Asians couldn't buy property here. I may not remember much of my life in China, but my family teaches me. My first lessons were about their importance."

"In the traditional Chinese home . . ." This is how Mina begins what she and Kenny call her "Chinese lessons." He explains, "We have these communication breakdowns not because of any language difficulties, but because we look at the world through different sets of cultural eyes." Mina teases him that he should have paid more attention in the Asian studies course that they all had to take in junior high.

Kenny tries to understand the Chinese concept of the family, that the family is the center of social life. He has to accept that Mina will suddenly leave to get home in time for dinner. "Among the Chinese, when possible, you go home for meals," she tells him, explaining how all food is individually stir-fried, cooked right then, never ahead of time and stored in a freezer.

Kenny also tries to understand why Mina isn't more sympathetic to his complaints about a lack of privacy. "Rather than coming right out and saying, 'Stop seeing Mina,' my mom started to limit my privacy. She'd suddenly decree that I couldn't stay in my room watching TV or listening to music. I had to sit in the den and study. 'I'm bored with school,' I say to her. So I'm fuming to Mina about how unfair this is. How am I to know that in Chinese there isn't even a word for 'privacy.' The closest translation is 'loneliness,' which is not at all what I meant."

Says Mina, "I explain that for the traditional Chinese, your identity lies in your past, and Kenny looks at me like I've said he shouldn't care about who he is now and in the future. He is missing my point. I was feeling guilty about not really respecting my parents by sneaking behind their backs." Kenny, on the other hand, began to pressure Mina to convince them to let her start dating. He also began to pressure her about having sex.

THERESA AND SCOTT

Then there is Theresa and Scott, with their own set of problems. She's trying to concentrate on her long-range goal of getting into Texas A & M where she'd like to major in psychology. Instead, she has "Scott on the brain." Theresa says, "I know if I don't pay attention to my grades and come up with good SAT scores, I'm not going anywhere." She describes her school as about "half and half, Anglo and Mexican," four hundred students, freshman through senior, with each one and their families minding everyone else's business. Theresa's business is that she happened to notice Scott.

"Even though he's two years ahead of me in school, we'd seen each other around. On the Fourth of July when I walked into U-To-Tem, that's like a 7-Eleven, who should be working there but Scott and a good friend of mine. I grabbed my friend and whispered, 'Introduce us, introduce us,' which he did. You see, Scott is extremely handsome and, I discovered later, smart as a whip. I was dying to go out with him . . . and the next thing I knew, he'd kind of asked me."

Within a month, Theresa and Scott decided they were each other's best friend. She made up every kind of excuse to stop by U-To-Tem. "Sure, my father laughed when I offered to go there to pick up some ice cream for my little sister—the same one who torments me. But all he said was 'Be careful.'" What Theresa didn't know at the time was that during one of her and Scott's clandestine meetings, his twenty-year-old sister happened to come into the store. Realizing that there seemed to be something going on between the two teens, she played detective. After seeing all she needed to see, she hurried home to make what she called her "hanky-pank report" to her mother.

"At the very beginning, when Scott's mother, Mrs. Miller, didn't know about our relationship, everything was calm," says Theresa. "And if I'd known from the start that he didn't want to tell her about me—or me about her—maybe I would never have gotten involved. My friend at U-To-Tem tried to warn me, 'Scott likes you, thinks you're cute, but he can't exactly date you.' When I asked him what that was supposed to mean, he told me, 'You're smart. You'll figure it out.'

"I didn't like the answer I came up with, that even though *I* consider myself an American, Mrs. Miller doesn't. To her, I'm Mexican, and since they're Anglo, she doesn't want us to date. Scott felt bad when I confronted him about it. He said, 'I don't want to hurt you, but you're right. I shouldn't see you anymore.' I asked him, 'Do I look too Mexican for you?' He answered, 'No, I don't even think about that. It doesn't matter to me.'"

It did matter to Mrs. Miller. She insisted that her son stop seeing Theresa. Her husband had died when Scott, the youngest of her children, was seven. He was her baby, her favorite. He wasn't going to turn into a troublemaker the way her older boy had. She wanted Scott's life under her control and planned out for him, and it didn't include a girl with a background like Theresa's. ("I'd never experienced this kind of prejudice before," says Theresa.)

To guarantee the end of their relationship, Mrs. Miller announced to Scott he would stay with his grandmother until his college classes started in two weeks. If he knew what was good for him, he'd be packed and ready to leave on the Houston-bound bus the next day. Within the hour, Scott made a furtive phone call to Theresa to let her know his mother's plan. "I can't leave without saying good-bye to you," he told her. "Stay there. I'll be over as soon as I can." Theresa and Scott spent the rest of the day together, first at the beach, then just driving around in his pick-up truck. By midnight, when they were parked in front of her house, they were both crying. They promised each other that they'd find a way to be together. At least,

Theresa should come to visit him at school for a weekend that fall.

"At that precise, romantic moment—our final good-bye—his sister pulls up in her car and Mrs. Miller pulls up in her car. They were there to bring Scott home! Right off, Mrs. Miller starts yelling all this terrible stuff: 'You're nothing but trash, Theresa, and Scott's trash for going out with you. There's lots of Mexican guys you can date.

"'I called your Anglo girlfriend's mother and told her I heard wicked tales about you. She shouldn't let her little girl hang around with you. You leave my son alone or I'll never let him return to the Valley. And if I *ever* see you two together, I'll get my gun and shoot the both of you!'

"'I was too afraid to be afraid, so I yelled right back, 'You do that and I'll call the police.'

"'I'd like to see you try that,' Mrs. Miller screamed. 'Don't you believe in the purity of the races?'

"Confused, I came back with something dumb like, 'What do you mean?'

"'You know, Mexicans dating Mexicans. Anglos dating Anglos.'

"'No, I don't believe in that,' I told her. 'It's what's inside that matters. How well you treat each other. What kind of person you are.' Mrs. Miller didn't want anybody 'interdating,' as she called it. So there she is dragging Scott away from me and hollering her head off, 'He's not going to see another dime toward college if he doesn't get rid of you.' And I'm hollering at Scott, 'Stand up to your mom or she'll wrap you so tight around her finger that you'll turn blue.'

"Then I'm back again hollering at Mrs. Miller, 'Mexican is not a race. Anglo is not a race. That's just your background. I was born in the same American hospital your son was. The only kind of race is the human race.' What I didn't say was, sure, my parents value their Mexican traditions and at times they say this country is too liberal. It takes too much for granted. But they also taught me that skin color doesn't matter.

"Right about then while I'm thinking all that, my father comes to check on all this commotion." Theresa describes her relationship with her father as not too close. ("If I had boy troubles, I couldn't talk to him. But, mainly, he doesn't want me to get hurt.") Seeing that Theresa was tremendously upset, he did his best to comfort her. "I saw his eyes were watering, and he suggested maybe I should give Mom a call over at the relative's where she was helping out."

Theresa's mother did what she could, listening to what happened and then teasing her daughter back into a more positive mood. She was sorry she'd missed all the excitement, the fun, and especially the chance to "lay into that wacko, Mrs. Miller." For the next three weeks, "an eternity," Theresa didn't hear a word from Scott. She felt "at the end of the road with no way to turn."

PARENTS' EQUAL TIME

These situations are told from the teenagers' points of view. Two representative parents agreed to share their views, to give adults some equal time. As Jonathan's father, Mr. Long, put it, in many conflicts there are often two sides—and then there's the truth. Like most parents, Mr. Long says his primary hope is that his son will be happy and healthy. But he knows that he's helping to raise a special child. Much as Jonathan's mother warned their son about interracial dating and the potential for prejudice, so has his father presented thoughts on that topic.

"As Jonathan was growing up, I tried to explain about prejudice. I remember telling him that even now, some twenty years after the civil rights movement, prejudice remains rampant. We still have a social system which is absolutely loaded with legacies of all the official racism that holds up white values as the norm. The 'white folks are the right folks' mentality.

"Prejudice also comes, I believe, from parents being worried about the image that's presented to their friends. Parents, I remind him, just like kids, want peer approval. They feel pressure to have their kids live right, go to the right school, date right, and eventually marry right.

"In our more recent talks, I let Jonathan know that while people may appear to be different, they all have the same kinds of emotions. They all need the same kinds of things to be happy. I tell him, Son, you need strokes and support from your friends and your lovers, no matter what your background. But if, when you find someone who really fits, you happen to cross a color barrier, what you've got to cope with is a lot of other people out there who won't agree. And, if you fly enough red flags in their faces, they will try to do something about it. Then it's up to you to figure out where you want to go from there. My hope is that you will find ways in your own life to be creative and good and fulfilled."

Mr. Long has been nothing but supportive of Jonathan's relationship with Heather.

Kenny, however, feels as if he's living with what he calls Mom-the-sniper. While she doesn't come out with direct attacks, she zings him with indirect actions. His mother, Mrs. Preston, agreed to share her side of the question in a phone interview one Friday afternoon. When asked what's happening with Kenny and Mina, she admits, "It's more what's happening to me," and then she laughs, somewhat embarrassed.

"I'm your basic WASP (white Anglo-Saxon Protestant), living in a WASP suburb. But even our school district has changed. Pasadena, the neighboring community, has always had a black community, but now around here there's a heavy influx of Chinese and also Mexicans. This is the melting pot of the future, and, suddenly, I'm the minority. Still, I was the very liberal, sixties mother who even dated a black, a man I was very much taken with for a long period of time.

"That's why my reaction to Kenny has taken *me* by surprise. Having been around all these people and every color kid forever, why should I catch my breath when my son starts dating one of them? Kenny's so unprejudiced that he wouldn't think twice about going out with a martian. The problem is more my inability to deal with this. I've tried to analyze why I'm upset, and this is what I've come up with.

"To start with, she is his first serious girlfriend. Of course, he's a very handsome boy; every mother thinks that. And he's always had a lot of friends, but this one I can see is turning into a romance. Maybe I'm reacting to that; no girl is ever good enough for a mother's son. Frankly, I think this one is a dud. A nothing. She is probably the only Chinese student who's flunking math. See, there I go, talking in stereotypes when I don't mean to. Anyway, when I first saw Mina, let's say I was taken aback that she was not blond and blue-eyed, which again is a reflection on me."

Then Mrs. Preston says she asked herself these questions: "What's really bothering me? What am I afraid of? Can I get beyond Mina's being Chinese? Can I make judgments based on my head and my heart? Do I really care what the neighbors might say? When I think, 'She's no good for him,' do I really mean, 'She's no good for me?'" Part of the job of being a parent, in Mrs. Preston's mind, is to create a supportive environment in which her son can grow. It is not to please the neighbors. On the other hand, she's from a small, central California town, and she carries forward "many small-town attitudes, of wanting things to be above reproach."

She tries, she says, to be calm about this relationship. She doesn't flat out say, "I forbid you to see her." Still, her body language is obvious. Consequently, she and Kenny have had arguments off and on for nearly six months. Even though they haven't specifically been about Mina, her guess is they are probably based on her own unvoiced anger and frustration. Kenny started lying to her, sneaking around and cutting class. He'd inform her that he was going over to one friend's house and when she'd call there, he would have never shown up. "I'm not strict," says Mrs. Preston, "but I do like to have a general sense of where he is."

As his mother, she believes she has a responsibility to know certain facts, including if he's sexually active. And if so, are they using suitable birth control? "Since he either clams up or leaves the room when I ask, I broached the topic one day when he and I were in the car. His response, after telling me it was none of my business, was to try to jump out while I was going fifty miles an hour and there's a car on my tail. The depth of his unhappiness or anger at me, whatever the emotion, was a shock.

"He's talking about my invading his privacy, while I'm worrying about where a racially mixed grandchild fits in to our life. My grandchild, that is. I only want to make Kenny's life's path as smooth as I can. No parent is sure how to factor in divorce and reconstituted families and what that all means and doesn't mean to our children. Instead of going over that ground again, what I suggest to Kenny is [for him to] consider his priorities. I say, 'Don't get so hung up on what's going on today that it will mess up what's going to happen five years from now.' I'm speaking from love for him, and he doesn't seem to get it. Since the incident in the car, though, I've just tried to let this relationship run its course."

4

BATTLE
PLAN

When you're involved in interracial or cross-cultural dating, those stars in your eyes can trigger parental explosions. To find out what those fireworks mean and how to limit them, we turned to a variety of experts for information. New York City therapist Ronny Diamond, M.S.W., is a faculty member at the Ackerman Institute for Family Therapy, and the director of the Spence-Chapin Adoption Counseling Team where, among other duties, she works with white couples who have adopted Korean children.

When asked what's behind those parental outbursts, Diamond led off the discussion by saying, "Parents expect that their children will follow the dating model that they have set out. And often that model is one of sameness, not difference. There are also families that very much value differences. In that environment, you can come home with a wide variety of people and each one is viewed as an individual.

"When you're dealing with the unknown, something new, however, it's often seen as scary. Dating someone of the same race and the same ethnic background, the same religion and the same world view, feels the most familiar and the most comfortable." Consequently, in our society, people tend to date and to marry within groups very much like their own. And of all those groups, crossing racial lines in particular remains the last taboo. In fact, not all that many years ago, it was illegal in certain southern states for those of different races to marry.

When it's a question of crossing cultural lines, these factors seem to relate. The less time your parents have lived in this country, the more they will feel foreign and potentially threatened by what they see around them. It's a tremendous shock to leave behind in the nation of your birth that which is familiar. During the years of adjustment, it's normal and natural to try to preserve your former culture. In addition, your parents may speak little or no English. They may decide that American child-rearing practices, including the amount of freedom many teenagers have, do not please them. The closer you and your parents match this profile, the more insistent they may be that if you date at all, it must be only those from a similar background. Parents generally are stricter if you, too, are foreign-born or first generation, rather than if you are second or third generation.

Concludes Diamond, "All parents, motivated by love, concern, and a deep desire to protect you, push for a course of action that they believe will lead to the fewest complications."

THE REINFORCEMENT
PHENOMENON

Parents' reactions to interracial or cross-cultural dating may sound insensitive and controlling to you. Some parents tell you that they themselves aren't against the dating; that they're not prejudiced. But because society isn't ready, they don't think it's a good idea at this time. You may hear that it's too hard to date someone who's different. And what will the neighbors and relatives think?

This may be the first in a series of escalating questions, with variations going something like the following. How could you think so little of yourself? How could you have no pride in your own culture? How could you do this to us, reject your parents? And then a warning similar to that given to Scott by his mother: "Don't you realize that if your grandmother ever finds out, this will kill her?"

If a verbal grilling turns sizzling, it means you have captured your parents' attention. Maybe you've never done that before. The family focuses on you. "Before this, sure, you could defy a curfew, or eat sweets when you weren't supposed to, but now we're talking about the big time," says Diamond. She explains that what you gain is dramatic: leverage and power and control.

When parents have a negative reaction, it underlines for you their belief that what's going on is significant. Psychotherapist Howells says, "Parents should know that the more they forbid a relationship, the more serious it's going to get." The negative reaction often gives the romance meaning it never would have had. This reinforcement, if frequent enough, results in you, the teenager, repeating the behavior. In other words, you keep dating the person who troubles your parents because of the new power it brings you at home. You may not be willing to give up the relationship and lose that control. Therapists call this whole process a reinforcement phenomenon.

Think about this. What if you don't really care very much for the person you're seeing? Telling your parents it's "true love" could be a cover for your attempt to stay in the family spotlight. Not that you plotted this event, but the result could be the same. Now consider this. When a relationship is maintained for that reason, your partner winds up being used and being turned into an object. That's not fair or right, and in a sense, it's exactly what prejudice is about. You see the object, not the person, which is as wrong as any parent's prejudice.

UNDERGROUND RELATIONS

What if your feelings are sincere? How can you turn your parents' negative reactions into positive ones? The experts admit that convincing them to let you date somebody who lacks their stamp of approval is a challenge. Their first rule, especially, may be the hardest: Don't go underground, don't continue to see each other in secret. Why not? Because the main focus of your time together is sneaking around. Instead of going out and having fun, you're busy plotting and lying.

Lynn E. Ponton, M.D., is a child and adolescent psychiatrist, and the director of the Adolescent Unit at the Langley-Porter Psychiatric Institute, University of California Medical Center in San Francisco. Routinely she sees people from ages twelve to twenty about problems ranging from depression to pregnancy to schizophrenia to interracial and cross-cultural dating. She says, "If the couple takes the relationship underground, in some ways it can become very romantic: us-against-the-world. What you lose, though, is the chance to experience the ordinary ups and downs of dating. Each contact has to be secretive. You have to go through all sorts of planning to get together. That spicy edge becomes exciting and may even be what binds you together." The battle against the parent becomes the issue; the ability to evaluate the relationship with any real honesty is lost in the shuffle.

IRENE AND RUBEN

Irene and Ruben, seniors at a large, integrated high school in Cincinnati, are discovering the reality behind those words. Although they are both U.S.-born, their backgrounds are complex. About one hundred years ago, Irene's relatives emigrated from India to South Africa, where they maintained their own quite conservative culture. Then, as newlyweds, her young parents immigrated to this country. As stated earlier, Ruben defines his heritage as Latino. His mother is originally from Puerto Rico, his father from Cuba. They met and married in New York City, moved to Miami, and eventually transplanted their growing family to its current home in Cincinnati.

When Irene and Ruben first started dating about five months ago, her parents had harsh words to say on the issue. "My mom saw us walking together and immediately said, 'Now, don't go get involved. That boy is a distraction.' Then she saw us again and said, 'Break it off'. So we tried," says Irene. "We stopped seeing each other except at school. And we never talked on the phone. When you really care for someone, though, it's hard not to be with him. He's my dream guy."

Ruben says, "It hurt me. I wanted to be accepted by her parents. I'd never done anything bad. I'd say to Irene, 'Why do they hate me?' I was rejected by her parents for something I couldn't do anything about. Their attitude made me feel like I was a lesser person."

Irene adds, "Because I love Ruben too much to lose him, on the sly we took up where we left off. And almost immediately my parents caught me." The first thing Irene was threatened with was being shipped off to relatives. "They said if I were to talk with, see, or have any dealings with Ruben, I would be sent to live with my mother's cousin. I didn't want to go, but I couldn't stop seeing Ruben. I kept lying and I kept being found out."

It is Ruben's opinion that Irene should sit down with her parents and tell them the truth. Her response is, "That's easier said than done." Still, Irene mentally plans just such a conversation, where she announces to her mother and father, "I am seeing Ruben and we are happy together. All my needs are being fulfilled. And if it's a mistake, that's how people learn." When she tries to say the words aloud, however, they come out sounding silly. "Every time I mention his name, there is like a wall between us that cannot be discussed." She and Ruben remain underground.

"What ends up happening, though, is that it's always crossing my mind when we're out together. What if my parents drive by? What if they see us? Yesterday we went to this fancy section of town called Kenwood where there are boutiques and little art galleries. I was supposed to call my mom at a certain time. When I did, no one answered. Ruben and I thought, she's out looking for me, which meant we both panicked."

At Christmas, when Irene stopped by Ruben's to exchange presents, her mother learned what she'd done. Once back home, she walked into the living room where she found her parents looking extremely somber. They didn't yell; rather, their manner was subdued. First Irene's mother, then her father, explained their position. They loved her and had faith in her. They wished they could trust her. They only had her best interests in mind. For lying, her punishment was a six-week grounding starting that moment and to include New Year's Eve. Irene worries about deceiving her parents. She admits that for a teenage girl from her culture, she has freedom. While she feels her relationship with her mother is suffering, she won't give up Ruben to improve it.

Irene's parents have never met Ruben. At one point, her mother said if Irene wanted him as a friend, all right. In America, her parents agree they shouldn't be able to pick her friends. He might be a nice boy, they say. Bring him home. Let them meet him. But thus far, Irene has not felt that her mother means it. So they have yet to see him on their doorstep, and her mother admits she can't imagine what would happen if he came to dinner. Irene's little brother would just be "all eyes and ears. He's always apt to say something that makes you want to kick him under the table."

Irene contends that once her mother did happen to see Ruben, and she gave him "awful looks." He's afraid to go over to their house. While he'd like to meet them, Ruben thinks Irene's parents would say something to him or react to something he said which would embarrass him or make him feel furious. So, it's a standoff.

THE NEXT LEVEL
OF SERIOUSNESS

Therapist Diamond says she's troubled when "both the kid and the parents know what's up and won't really deal with it. When the parents are willing to look the other way, that means the burden is on the adolescent; and that's too big a burden. The parents are giving the message—we don't want to deal with that, and the kid is probably following this lead. My suspicion is, in a situation like that, if you were to bring it up, you'd probably meet with a lot of flack from the parent. This is too disturbing, so don't disturb us."

What concerns Dr. Ponton about parents who don't want to deal with these situations is that "to strike back at them, you may wind up hurting yourself much more. The dating might be part of a series of destructive actions. In addition, you may carry this issue to the next level of seriousness, pregnancy. And that becomes the grave life choice that it shouldn't have to be."

At thirteen, Susan, of Polish descent, began having trouble with crack; so much, in fact, that her parents checked her into a residential program for a couple of months. At fourteen, she informed her mother and father that she was pregnant and had no intention of having an abortion. Her mother tried to persuade her to have one, but Susan refused. She went away to a home for unwed mothers where, prior to deciding on adoption, she was made to name and hold the child. At that point, Susan's Bahamian boyfriend said he was no longer interested in being involved.

A Costa Rican–born American teenage girl chose to raise her biracial child, moving in with an older sister, her husband, and their three-year-old. A Taiwanese-American girl, abandoned by her white boyfriend, felt abortion was her best answer. In the hospital unit where Dr. Ponton works, she sees many "problems with pregnancies from mixed racial and cultural dating. There have been cases where the girl has hidden the pregnancy from the family up until delivery. And cases where the girl is disowned by the boy, and if she tries to get help from her family, she hears, 'We told you he was bad. We said it would never last.' What I suggest is the girl try to get the support from a female figure in her family. There is usually an understanding sibling, an aunt, or maybe a grandmother who'll come through."

AVERTING A CRISIS

Therapists report that parents have a tendency to jump ahead, to envision you married to this person you're currently dating. When your child marries, they say, he or she is marrying into a family. Your child's going to have in-laws and they're going to be part of your family. If it's not someone from your own culture, that's going to be uncomfortable. Then—the hidden fear, especially in interracial situations—what about the children, these parents say. How will future grandchildren deal with society and how will society deal with them?

Before you and your parents get to that crisis point, there are steps you can take to try to work through these problems. For instance, you might invite your parents to a school function—maybe a football game, or a dance, or an open house. If they don't speak much English, maybe there's a bilingual family friend who can go along to act as a translator. Suggest they go to a P.T.A. meeting, or call the guidance counselor, the librarian, or a teacher and find out what's what at your school. What is *their* opinion of your partner? Is he or she okay? And how are *you* doing, for that matter?

Dr. Ponton says, "Your parents may not have realized how integrated your school is, especially when compared to what they're familiar with—more segregated neighborhoods. In this setting, they're encouraged to see whom you're dating as part of your crowd, a human being, not a stereotype." Eventually, they might begin to understand that your attraction isn't such a mystery. This person is also liked by your friends and a valued member of the student body. (If that's not the case—your partner is a lowlife—you should consider why you want to be with a loser, race and background aside.)

For an alternative, you could invite some of your friends over, including the one whom you think is special. Again, in this kind of neutral, unpressured environment, your parents might notice that she or he doesn't have fangs. Later, when you mention you're dating, they might recall their original positive impression, before resorting to any lectures or feeling threatened. You *can* reason with most parents.

"If nothing has worked, if your parents are refusing to go to school activities, if they don't want you to have over teens from other backgrounds, then you have no choice but to discuss it with them," says Dr. Ponton. "And it *is* going to be a difficult talk, or series of talks." The therapists concur, however, that it's worth pursuing if you want the romance to continue. Perhaps talking with someone at one of the many interracial organizations might help. When parents are involved in your life, they will be more sympathetic toward any attraction, even one that they might call a rebellion. At the very least, they will appreciate being informed.

BATTLE TACTICS

Don't begin any discussion of this issue by screaming at each other. If your parents have just learned of your relationship, or if they just caught you breaking one of their dating rules, therapists suggest it's best for everyone to hold off on reacting. Wait until tempers cool and everyone is calmer. You should agree to go over what's happening in your life at a preplanned kid-adult meeting. You might even want to prepare an agenda, and if the bodies are available, have someone take notes. Once it's time to talk, you should be willing to listen to your parents' way of thinking, just as you'd like them to listen to yours.

Psychotherapist Howells says, "Parents owe it to you to have reasons other than just the person's race or culture for why they don't want you to see each other. And you owe it to them to realize that the person's racial or ethnic background may *not* be what they object to." There's the example of a Native American teenager from Milwaukee. When she was fourteen, she began dating a twenty-year-old white high school dropout who'd served time in jail for armed robbery. Her mother insisted that it was the age difference, the prison record, and the young man's questionable future that concerned her. The daughter, on the other hand, refused to consider that the mother was anything but racist.

"When parents take a strong stand, you feel you have to counteract with an equally strong stand," says therapist Diamond. "And that doesn't leave room for negotiation, for you to really think about what you want. All the energy goes into convincing the other that he or she is wrong. Maybe your parents lay down an ultimatum—stop the relationship. You're thinking, You can't make me because I'm an adult now. Then you do the opposite just to show them that they can't force you to do something against your will. Meanwhile, you're upset, angry, and hurt, as are your parents. They are feeling, Our child is too young to know what's best in this situation. He/she lives in a dream world and doesn't understand the reality of life. What's wrong with our parenting? They may have a sense of guilt or a sense of shame."

This might be the right point at which to try to understand why your parents have their particular point of view. Find out what their beliefs are that lead them to forbid this kind of relationship. What is it that they are uncomfortable about? What do they believe is dangerous about the situation? What do they think it will reflect on you, their child? What do they think it will say to the world?

Psychiatrist Ponton states, "Parents may perceive your actions as a rejection of them and the kind of life they're providing. In some situations, they might fear that your relationship will drop your social status. Often, though, they have an underlying conflict that isn't so much about dating. It's about sex. And sex is never easy to discuss. A girl's parents could worry that their daughter is sexually active. The conversation then becomes more than one about interracial or cross-cultural dating. It might include the topics of birth control, condoms, and barrier protection. Your parents may fear that even if you don't become pregnant, you could get some sexually transmitted disease. You could develop the AIDS antibodies. They may see this as the time to talk about AIDS and AIDS testing, a topic on which they may be poorly informed."

During your turn to speak, explain your point of view. You might say that you feel you have a right to date who you like. You want to be open and honest; you don't want to lie. You don't think it's going to be helpful to you to stop seeing the person just because they say so. It would be more helpful, you feel, if you come to that realization on your own.

If you're doing well in other parts of your life—your grades, attendance at school, and attitude—remind your parents of that fact. If you believe the relationship is fine, not self-destructive, tell them so. Finally, ask if there is any bargaining position, a compromise, a second round of talks that could be scheduled. With persistence and patience may come a payoff.

SARA AND BENIGNO (BENNIE)

Persistence and patience paid off for Staten Island, New York, resident, Sara. She is white, and her boyfriend, Benigno—Bennie—is Filipino. In this case, her parents were less than enthusiastic when he started "hanging around" their daughter. "My mom especially couldn't see me going out with someone from another culture," says Sara, now sixteen. She sometimes wonders whether her mother's reaction would have been muted if Bennie, eighteen, had simply had lighter skin. But he doesn't, and the day-to-day struggle with her mother continued for a year of negotiations before it began to improve.

"At first my mother simply hated my seeing him. She didn't accept it," says Sara. "When she began haunting me to break up with him, I would answer, 'I can't see what's so terrible about it.' She'd reply, 'What happens if you marry him? There are enough problems in the world without your adding a half-and-half kid to the population.' When my mother would start in like that, I admit it, I'd talk back, then disappear into my room. From my side of the closed door, you could hear my parting shot, 'This relationship is not going to last forever. Leave us alone!' That response was greeted by Mom's silence.

"What bothered me, too, was that I didn't tell Bennie about any of this. Sure, he knew something was wrong, but I couldn't bring myself to say, 'You know my mother, the sweet-faced woman with the curly hair who smiles when you come over? Well, she's a racist. . . . ' His parents really like me, so how come it couldn't be the same with mine, I'd wonder."

After Sara and her mother repeated their arguments with all their variations, Sara turned to a different tactic.

She realized that denying her mother any real knowledge of her life was stupid. It was no big deal to offer more details than she had in the past about her classes, teachers, and friends and an edited version of what she and Bennie did in their spare time.

Her mother, for her part, was more than willing to listen. Sara says, "I'd stress that we were not carrying on some secret relationship. We weren't hanging out in the city, looking to get into trouble. I wasn't coming home loaded or smashed. We usually went out in a group, the two of us and a few friends, like a couple of my girlfriends and a friend of his. We went to the mall, bowling, to an under-twenty-one place to dance; fun, but not exactly the wild social life. I explained to my parents that we were doing nothing that would embarrass them in front of their friends."

In the middle of a conversation on this topic, Sara's mother might shift gears and suddenly say, "You're a good-looking girl. You're bright and outgoing. If you'd put Bennie on the back burner, you wouldn't have any problems coming up with dates."

How would Sara reply? "He's somebody I can talk to. He's my really good friend. There are things I can say to him that I can't say to anybody else. And *he* is the one who encourages me to study. If I brought home a failure, that's another story." (Sara, who hopes to become a paralegal or a lawyer, maintains about an 85 average. She works two nights a week for a law firm. She is earning her own spending money while gaining valuable knowledge. How bad an influence could Bennie be?)

Sara enlisted her four younger sisters to help. Without much prompting, they started telling their mother that, in their opinion, Benigno was nice; they liked him. The neighbors in the all-white section where they live started getting used to seeing him come around. Each day Sara and Bennie walked to school together, then had English and lunch the same period. They talked on the phone daily and went out on weekend nights. "This is serious, for now," became Sara's refrain.

Then one Saturday evening, while Sara was still trying to decide what to wear on their date, she overheard her mother asking Bennie his plans for the future. Since her mother usually kept Bennie at an emotional distance, Sara took this sign as a small victory. She could hear Bennie's voice, with its hint of an accent, as he explained that he was looking at universities with good sports medicine programs. There was a small school in North Carolina and one called Westchester in Pennsylvania he was particularly interested in. "That's wonderful," Sara's mother replied, perhaps relieved, because she knew Sara wanted to attend Hunter College in Manhattan, hundreds of miles away from either college.

"Lately, my mother asks more about the way Bennie treats me. 'That's what's important,' she says. 'Is he good to you?' A friend of hers asked her a few weeks ago how she felt about Bennie. I nearly flipped when I heard her say, 'To tell you the truth, I like him a lot. He's a cute kid.'

"Sure, I know she's riding it out until he leaves for college. She even mentioned in one of those offhand ways that mothers have how this friend of hers saw a magazine survey. News bulletin: ninety percent of *all* high school romances fizzle by Christmas when the two people go to separate schools. Because of 'exposure to a new environment,' the relationship lasts only three to four months before it dissolves. 'Thanks, Ma,' I told her, and we both laughed. I'm the oldest. By the time they get to the baby of the family, she'll be able to date a guy who's purple and it'll go unnoticed."

5

BORDERING ON
TROUBLE

There's no denying it. Relationships that add the extra dimension of crossing racial or cultural lines often border on trouble. The greater the visual difference, the more these special couples are noticed and create societal ripples in a way that others just don't. That means not only do you have all the regular stuff with which any couple has to cope, you also have to confront the results of your challenging what much of society dictates as "normal" and "right." This fallout can go far beyond irritating a parent. Other people in and around your world may come down on you, too.

How do friends and classmates view interracial or cross-cultural dating? It depends a lot on the school, which, in turn, reflects the area from which it draws students and staff. For those of you from, for instance, Vermont towns and cities, the issue of meshing races and cultures is frequently more theoretical. According to the latest census figures, out of a population of more than half a million, there were 1,135 blacks and fewer still Latinos and Asians. Others of you, however, live in more integrated environments where the black, Latino, and Asian populations are more substantial.

Suburbs across the land are gradually growing more integrated, too. Twenty-five years ago in Montgomery County, Maryland, next to Washington, D.C., the junior and senior high school population was overwhelmingly white. Today the same classrooms reveal a far broader racial and cultural spectrum. For those from inner cities, such as New York's Lower East Side, dealing with a rich blend of people is a way of life. At a single intersection, Madison and Rutgers streets, near the Manhattan Bridge, you're surrounded by multiple cultures where at least four separate languages are spoken: English, Chinese, Spanish, and Hebrew.

If there's racial harmony in the community you call home, fine; there will be a carryover to what happens at your school. But currently in America, good race relations are the exception, not the rule. With the number of violent racially motivated incidents continuing to soar, the prejudice, anger, and hate behind them aren't magically left outside the classroom door. The same holds true for any ethnic divisions.

Inside the schools of America it often looks quite different from your parents' day. Now, Boston public schools are 63 percent black and Latino; Chicago schools are 83 percent black and Latino; Houston, 81 percent; Los Angeles, 75 percent; Miami, 75 percent; New York, 72 percent; and St. Louis, 76 percent.[1] The Asian population has increased substantially, too, with sizable communities in Chicago, Houston, Los Angeles, Miami, New York, San Diego, and San Francisco.

Some inner-city and private schools remain segregated or with only a small number of different students. Even in well-integrated schools, individual classes may be pretty solidly one race. The college prep or advanced placement classes might be filled only with whites or, in some

East and West Coast schools, primarily with Asians. Behind closed doors, you often segregate yourselves—in the cafeteria, the auditorium, wherever you're allowed to choose where to sit. All this can translate into an undercurrent of tension, a muffled rage waiting for a reason to explode.

Into this atmosphere strolls that "different" couple. Walking down the hall. Holding hands in assembly. Hanging out by the lockers. Passing notes in history. These all might be routine activities for a couple at school, but not always for the interracial or cross-cultural one. You never really know if someone might zing you: Hey "bogo" or "whitey" or "beaner" or "gook." "Get out of my face. I don't like the two of you together." What comes next? Do you pull out guns and shoot each other? Or maybe knives and chains? Do you vanish? Ignore what was said? Try to discuss the matter?

JONATHAN AND HEATHER

Jonathan and Heather in their own way had to contend with these facts. Away from the dramatic peaks and sunsets of Nevada, neither of them felt that comfortable when envisioning meeting the other's friends. For Jonathan, Heather represented a type of female he doesn't care for and, to an extent, even resents. He calls them "princesses," "snobs," and "self-centered brats." Heather admits that were they to attend the same school, they'd have different sets of friends. "We don't talk about it outright, but we both know that's true."

With Jonathan's visit to Philadelphia looming, Heather realized the time had come to let her best friend, Jennifer, hear the whole story. "I was afraid of her reaction to his being black," says Heather. "Actually, I was concerned about how all my friends would react. Jennifer would never consider going out with a black person ever in her entire life, even if she were in my situation. While I wouldn't call her a racist, I knew there would be no perfect moment to bring this up." Now, months later, Heather still remembers the day in Jennifer's Toyota, driving along, and trying to ease into this announcement.

"I was telling her, 'You have to meet Jonathan. He's really a sweetheart and smart. He's got a kind of flattop haircut and an adorable, lopsided grin. He lives in a neat townhouse with his mother and stepfather. And . . . and . . . what I'm avoiding is that he's . . . half black.'

"'Really?' Jennifer said. Just that one word, 'Really.' I knew she didn't know how to accept it; that she didn't want to sound like it mattered. But it did, especially since it wasn't anything my friends were doing."

The next hurdle was when Heather and Jonathan went to a party given by Heather's group of friends. They walked in, and she said, "Hey, guys, this is Jonathan!" After everyone exchanged assorted "hi's" and "how are you's," her friends went back to their conversations, assuming Jonathan was not *the* Jonathan Heather had mentioned so often. This Jonathan, after all, was black. Jonathan recalls the event as one of his least favorite evenings. "We left when one of her girlfriends said she was sick of dating blond guys. She wanted them dark. And someone answered, 'Talk to Heather. She likes her guys really dark.'"

Heather's turn to meet on Jonathan's turf came on a crisp Friday in mid-October. On the train down to Washington to meet his family and friends, Heather realized she was nervous. When Jonathan met her at the station, they opted for humor as their best weapon against the tension and apprehension they both felt. Jonathan joked, "My friends won't hold it against you that you're white. They're sophisticated and come from a mix of racial and ethnic groups."

"It's interesting that his friends turned out to be so unlike mine," states Heather. "Since this is the best relationship I've ever had, it makes me question the type of people I've been hanging out with. I sometimes wonder if maybe Jonathan's a better person because he *has* been through so much in his life. Has that made him more understanding?''

Even though Jonathan now stresses that Heather's friends are much warmer and more open with him, sometimes he still calls her school pep rallies "Klan meetings.'' On one of his weekend visits to Heather's Philadelphia neighborhood, they teased each other. "Check it out; there's actually another black person on the street!'' They both admit that not in Washington but in Philadelphia, "people look at [us] funny.'' Jonathan says that it's a racist city, and he feels unsafe in many sections of it. Heather adds that she's been forbidden by her parents to be out late with Jonathan on weekend nights. "I get into fights with them about that. They're afraid that some drunks might say something, which they probably would. And that's really a bummer.''

What's a bummer, too, is the periodic sense of isolation that nearly all these couples report feeling. While you don't walk around in a state of perpetual gloom, being a different kind of couple from an estimated 85 percent of your classmates has to touch you. It may well make you feel alone, even together.

With Kenny and Mina from Los Angeles, the problem often stems from Mina's double identity. She's not a native-born citizen, while most of the other Asian heritage classmates are second, third, and even fourth generation. Consequently, she doesn't always feel a strong identification with their world, and none at all with Kenny's. This results in the couple's spending most of their free time together alone, not with friends. With Irene and Ruben from Cincinnati, however, the majority of their friends have been supportive, as have been Sara's and Bennie's on Staten Island.

STARES AND GLARES

According to Bennie, their high school of four thousand students has a growing Filipino population. "There are about fifty just in the senior class. But to be honest, at school we are part of a special world. Out *there,* we know, is different. We think mixed dating is acceptable. Our friends do too. While we're comfortable with it, we're seeing that that doesn't carry over to the rest of the world."

All the couples brought up situations where they've been stared at or hassled. With Irene and Ruben, the experience was almost a worst-case scenario.

Although Irene doesn't wear the traditional Indian sari, nor does she paint a *bindi,* the small dot symbolic of unity and love, on her forehead, she and Ruben ran into racial trouble one day. They met an older Indian woman, a family acquaintance, who was dressed in a sari. As they stood and talked, Irene's big worry was whether this woman would tell Irene's parents that she had seen their daughter. The three of them didn't see the approaching gang of about ten. Suddenly, they were surrounded, kicked, shoved, and terrorized by chants of "dotbusters," a reference, they later figured out, to the Indian bindi. It was over as quickly as it began, when the gang scattered at the sound of an unrelated police siren. "Even though we were all shaken up," says Irene, "that incident had little to do with Ruben and me being together. Instead, it only showed how ugly prejudice is."

Interracial or cross-cultural couples can serve as lightning rods for trouble. "There is fighting among teens, and a lot of that is centered around issues of sex and mixed dating," says Dr. Ponton, a psychiatrist. "It will start out with obscene words referring to each other's racial or ethnic characteristics, including the way you look—your face. From there the level of violence can escalate to assault or even murder."

How might you handle these disturbing occasions? Experts suggest that you may have to make choices about where the two of you go together. If you know that a certain section of town or a particular event could make you feel conspicuous, at the least, or be dangerous, at worst, you have choices. Decide if you really want or need to go, and if not, skip it. You don't need to prove anything to anybody.

If you're stared at or glared at, it will probably bother you. Dr. Ponton says that first you have to consider that the looks might be from curiosity. "A Japanese-American girl with a long-time relationship with a Caucasian boyfriend said that it took her three years to accept and recognize the fact that they would be stared at, and that those stares could be for positive reasons.

"Throughout these potentially uncomfortable moments, keep in mind that this relationship is something you've chosen to do. You're proud of it and feel it's okay. While you could return the stare, focus some of the embarrassment on the person who directs it your way, you're better off to ignore it, pretend to be oblivious to what's going on. If the incident seems to be heating up, sooner rather than later, find help."

If you know the person who's making you feel lousy, you could always respond in a friendly manner. Try, for instance, "Susie, Jimmy, have you met my friend Carole? We're on our way to the mall. Why not come along?" By bringing politeness and interaction into the event, you might reduce the possibility of danger.

What can you do if someone asks you up front, "How can you date someone that different?" An acceptable answer is, "It's none of your business." Beyond that, you could throw that person a curve, responding, "Does mixed dating bother you? Why do you think that happens? Has this always been a problem for you? Have you considered seeking help to resolve your conflict on this issue?" By then, the person who's tried to ruin your day should have disappeared along with any battle.

TURN ME LOOSE

Even without direct confrontation, the evidence of prejudice mounts until many of you think twice before turning your hearts loose. A white teenager from Millington, Michigan, admits, "Before I met this guy, I swore up and down I'd never get myself involved with black people for more than just friends. With him, though, my feelings changed completely around. He is so sweet and makes me feel so good inside. But where we live is too small a town to make it all right for me to see him. I pulled the plug before the lights really went on. But, I'm having a tough time giving myself a reason why I had to do that."

One of the few black students at a Des Moines, Iowa, suburban high school was informed by a teacher, "You're a big football player now. If you want the community to be on your side, don't get involved with white girls." What the guy had done was kid around with some students, including a white cheerleader. When he arrived home furious, his mother's suggestion was "to keep being friends and try to wait it out—don't date—until college. Things will change then." "That's unnatural," he grumbled.

A black teenager from Gadsden, South Carolina, found herself attracted to a white classmate. She ignored her emotions. A white teenager from Miami, Florida, with prompting from a cousin, got up the courage to call the boy she really likes. "Is he ever cute!" she says, before admitting that because he's Cuban, most of their relationship takes place over the phone. "A lot of the kids at school are racist," she says. "They'll use white as an insult, like 'to hell with all those wormy white people,' 'cause most of the teachers are white. It doesn't feel good, but you get used to it." A Mexican-American and a black who are tenth-grade students in Albuquerque, New Mexico, say that their "relationship stays under complete secrecy." If their friends found out about it, they might be turned into outcasts. Discussions about "going public" only make them depressed.

For Michelle, a white tenth grader at a rural county high school on Maryland's eastern shore, any romance with Thomas, who's black, was destined to fail. Echoing the sentiments of many teens, she says these relationships often go nowhere because of this recurring fear: What will others think? "I worry about other people's opinions of me. That's the type of person I am," she says. When discussing the issue with an older married sister, she heard, "It's not right, so forget it. If God had meant for the races to mix, He wouldn't have made us all different colors."

KELLY AND RANDALL

For all the trouble these couples may experience, there's also talk of positive trade-offs. Consider Kelly and Randall from Dunwoody, Georgia. They came across each other in tenth grade the day the swim team was competing for the county championship. Kelly, who's white, noticed Randall, who's black, cheering for her from the far side of the pool. After she came in third, he approached- her, offering congratulations along with his phone number.

"He said, 'Call me,' and I said, 'Yeah, right,' kind of sarcastically. But a few days later I realized we were in the same Algebra II class; I gave him my number. When he called that night, and then kept on calling, we just had the greatest time talking. My last boyfriend felt inferior to me because I was athletic and he wasn't. He was trying to compete. With Randall, we both love sports and we have our own things that we're good at."

Now seniors, these two have watched their relationship grow and deepen. Because of the bond they feel with each other, they chose an emotional compromise to try to work within Kelly's parents' rule. Kelly explains, "We can see each other at a school function, but Randall can't come to my home, pick me up, and take me.

"My parents say, 'Society considers that a date and you and Randall can't date.'" Randall disagrees with this situation, but for Kelly's sake he is trying to hold his temper. "I tell her," says Randall, 'Kelly, you've got to stop and realize we're looking at the 1990s. There's more mixing of people than you first believe.' And she knows, the more you look, the more you see."

Kelly says of the twenty-five hundred students at their eighth-through-twelfth-grade integrated school, "I don't think there's that much prejudice." What would happen if she went to the prom with Randall? "I think it would be fine, except my parents wouldn't allow it. They tell me I'd feel embarrassed if the neighbors saw us together. But people at school are always saying how cute Randall and I are together. We're always play-fighting. No one there would think anything about it."

Kelly's girlfriends know about the relationship and are supportive. They're glad that she has somebody to talk to when she needs it. "The teachers," says Kelly, "like him, too. Why only the other day, a teacher mentioned that we really seem to have fun together. She did wonder, though, how the black girls feel about my being close to Randall."

When this subject came up before with Randall, he admitted that some of the black girls didn't like Kelly. "It comes down to the fact I'm white and good friends with him," says Kelly. "I guess they're resentful and feel in a way that I'm taking him from them. But my girlfriends and I would probably feel the same if the situation were reversed, if one of 'our guys' dated a black girl."

Randall states, "I don't have any interest in other girls. I've got Kelly to talk to and do stuff with. She's special. No matter what happens, I don't ever want to lose contact with her, and she knows that. We've now known each other for over two years. Our friends are the same, in the same clique. We've been in the same classes, worked together on projects. We care about all of us doing well. And that's what's going to turn this world into an integrated place, not just plunking us down in some school together and saying, 'Now, you all, get along.'"

Other interracial and cross-cultural couples agree with Randall's positive outlook. They have the fun and romance any two people do, and then something extra. They tell stories about the unique parts of their relationships that counter the rocky times. Kenny and Mina, among others, feel they've gained specific knowledge about each other's heritage. States Kenny, "Once when I had a cold, Mina brought me this great herbal treatment her mother uses. I told her that next she was going to force me to see an acupuncturist, which she agreed might not be a bad idea. And even though I'm not religious, through Mina I've learned about her religion, Buddhism."

Theresa from Texas says that despite "Scott's mother being a brick wall, by going through the rough spots together, I think Scott and I feel more united and stronger as a couple. What helped, too, was I went and talked with my school counselor. She was understanding and also honest. She told me that in situations like mine, where a guy's parent doesn't want them to see each other, it might not really be my choice anymore. She worked with me to reason through why I wanted to be with him. Had it become a fight to see who was in charge of Scott's life?"

Heather speaks for many of these couples when she says that because of her feelings for Jonathan, she'll never be able to view any race or cultural relations with her previous detachment. She's much more aware of, sensitive to, and knowledgeable about these issues. She now sees the individuals, not just the labels. And today her friends respect and admire her for doing something special: recognizing a person's worth based on what's inside, not on externals like skin color.

6

ARE YOU CRAZY

OR WHAT?

Did you ever wonder why you're attracted to one person and not another? Well, when it comes to two teens' mutual attraction, even the people who study human behavior admit they don't really know for sure. It's a topic that hasn't been studied. What they do know, however, is this: During the early years of adolescence—twelve, thirteen, fourteen—if you're dating someone quite different, from another race or a great deal older, for instance, parents can and should have influence over your choices.

IDENTITY FORMATION

For the middle to older range of teenagers, fourteen to eighteen or nineteen, however, something special is happening and parents ought to remember that fact. By this age, you're trying to figure out who you are in relation to your parents. Where do your ideas fit in with theirs, and how are you a separate and independent person? And it's tricky for you to be able to judge whether you *are* independent thinkers. If you feel exactly the same way as your parents, how do you know you're not just listening to them? How do you know you are coming up with your own ideas? This is what testing is all about. Your life becomes one of experimentation in every area, dating included. The therapeutic community even gives this stage a name: the age of identity formation.

Here's the crunch. During this identity formation, a guaranteed method of measuring yourself against your parents is by dating someone who you know goes against their values. Jump that invisible racial or cultural barrier and a parent's show of concern and/or prejudice can be added to the normal teenage struggle to become an independent adult. Since civilization began, or at least since Romeo's and Juliet's respective parents refused to let them see one another, many parents have felt it's part of their responsibility to regulate dating. But whom you choose to associate with is one of the things they find hardest to control.

"Basically, whom you choose to date isn't all that different from, say, how you choose to look," therapist Diamond asserts. She offers the example of the mother in elegant silks, the father in the pin-striped suit, and the daughter with spiked hair and pants so tight she has to use pliers to zip them. The issue remains the same: your experimentation. At this time, if your parents say the wheel is round, you're likely to say it's square. What this verbal sparring represents is a very natural part of your life where you begin to separate emotionally from your parents to prepare yourself to eventually leave home. In fact, therapists say that's what the task of adolescence is all about. In the process, parents may claim that you are driving them crazy.

At the height of emotions, parents forget that you are in another developmental stage, such as the stage when two-year-olds make "no" their favorite word. Instead, what they train their sights on is your "antagonistic behavior." Psychotherapist Howells advises, "They forget that it is an age to try on different ideas for size, to see how they fit. Parents have a tough time watching you—their adorable, cuddly kid—going off with confidence in a direction that they are sure is doomed. And, indeed, your relationship may well fail. Or, you may surprise your parents. They, too, may learn from this dating situation."

PATHOLOGICAL =
EMOTIONAL PROBLEMS

What your parents might more readily remember is that when they were your age, interracial dating was often viewed as not only wrong, but as pathological as well. The teenager who dated across racial lines had emotional problems. Therapist Diamond explains that "in the sixties, the feeling was that it was mostly liberal, white, middle-class girls going out with black dudes, so to speak; blacks who were not middle class. There was a sense that those kinds of girls didn't value themselves very highly. They had poor self-esteem. It had to do with the concept of 'dating or marrying down.'"

For some, interracial dating in the 1960s was also a political act—these young people felt it showed they believed in equality. In that era, therapists, psychologists, and psychiatrists wore blinders of sorts. While looking mostly at black and white couples, they failed to consider this point: If this behavior were judged pathological for the white female, what about the black male she was dating? "It was not seen as pathology, because it's often stepping more into the mainstream," says Diamond. "In the man's own minority group, however, it would be seen as a lack of pride in one's racial identity."

Today when a white female dates a minority male, do therapists continue to see it as evidence of pathology? Some do and some don't. While Diamond wishes this belief had changed, she's not convinced it has. What still seems to hold true, though, is that nationwide interracial as well as cross-cultural couples are a bit more likely to involve a white female and a minority male. Why? Dr. Ponton guesses that this might be occurring "simply because white females have more freedom. Asian and Hispanic females, for instance, generally have a lot stricter rules when it comes to dating."

WHAT'S THE ATTRACTION?

Dr. Ponton states that in exploring the underlying reasons for your dating choices, psychiatrists now try to focus on helping you question and find out your own meaning. "They don't have some preconceived notion that dating blacks or whites or whatever is bad. Mostly they're concerned about why you're doing what you're doing."

Ask Heather what attracts her to Jonathan and she'll tell you she's never met anyone like him before. "At first, at camp, when he'd say things like, 'I love you,' I'd say, 'You can't be serious.' I figured I'd never see him again. Then once we got home and I talked to him on the phone, I started thinking about him and how much fun we had.

"He really *cares* about a lot of things. Like one summer he did community service for some town he'd never heard of simply because he feels it's important to help others. So many people feel that to be cool you shouldn't get excited about stuff. Not Jonathan. He has opinions. With him, life is an adventure. He's sensitive and gentle. He's just so much a better person than my old boyfriend, Max, that it made good sense to dump him [Max] for Jonathan. And the most special thing about Jonathan is that he cares for me so much."

What attracts Irene and Ruben to each other? What makes her risk keeping his picture by her bed? Irene says, "We're love, warmth, and companionship for each other. I feel better when he's near. I'm here for him and he's there for me. He's always joking around, acting cute.

I love his personality. Whenever I have a problem, he has a different way to solve it. There's not any of that typical guy stuff, 'Duhh, I dunno.' And if I tell him something, he never goes and tells other people. I trust him completely."

Ruben's feelings for Irene are equally strong. "If something were to happen to her, I don't know what I'd do. The other day when I had a problem with one of my teachers, Irene was the person I had to tell first; not my parents, and I'm close to them. I feel protective of her even though I know she's strong. When she goes through these battles with her folks, I always try to make sure that she's all right. She says another guy might tell a girl, 'I don't want to mess with this.' But I try to help her. Irene's an amazing person, one of a kind. She makes me feel good about myself."

What matters to Sara about Bennie is that "aside from the fact he's a real cutie, he has his priorities on straight. He's always letting me know that I'm important, but he also values more, I suppose you'd call them, adult goals. He's my personal cheerleader, always after me about keeping up my grades. He's real encouraging about looking at my part-time job as experience for my career. On top of that, his image is good. His style is to wear a black trench coat, a man's hat—a fedora—and a lot of baggy gray clothes in layers. He's just a whole lot of fun and a fabulous dancer."

Kenny likes Mina "because she's different." He feels she came along at a good time. "I'd been getting bored with school, and I was tired of my mom treating me like a kid. So there I am in biology class and Mina was sure more interesting than some dead frog. She's pretty, sexy, and good to talk to. She listens to my problems. She's willing to take chances to be with me and show that she likes me. With only being able to see her at school and afterward at my house, it's kind of like having a secret friend. That makes it exciting."

Besides their love of sports, Randall and Kelly came up with a long list of things that bring them together. As with many of the other couples, they mention looks, style, and a sense of humor all near the top. "He reminds me of Theo in 'The Cosby Show,'" says Kelly. "You see, my last boyfriend was the type who's nice to you when or if he likes you, nasty when he doesn't. With Randall, there's this basic goodness going on. I know whatever happens, we'll always be friends."

Randall adds, "Kelly knows why I like her and that's what's important. I get embarrassed giving any more details to others about it."

Theresa is attracted to Scott because he's good-looking, as well as everything else she's ever wanted in a boyfriend. "I don't stick with him because he's a challenge, even though he's popular and could date any girl he wanted to. He treats me real good. He's polite. He has it all together and is more mature than the guys in my class. I consider him a man, and the others, they're just boys. I love hearing about college and what he's doing there."

Is this the first time Scott's gone against his mother's wishes and dated a Mexican-American? "No," says Theresa, "he's done it before and the same thing happened. His mother went bonkers. It's okay for him to date Anglos, but he told me that Anglo girls just aren't as much fun for him."

IS IT A PATTERN?

Sometimes therapists are troubled by what it might mean if a teen is *only* attracted to someone who's different. Take the situation with Kate, for example. This eleventh grader started high school outside of Detroit, and then last year moved with her family to Kansas City. She explains that since she was fourteen, even though she's white, all her boyfriends have been black. Kate told her mother about her first black boyfriend, Jack. "She said I couldn't see him. A mixed relationship was not accepted in society, according to Mom. Jack and I continued to be great friends, talking on the phone often, and then just before I moved, we had sex."

Part of getting used to her new school was "checking out the fellows," Kate says. "I met a couple who I really liked, then I fell in with a black senior name Philly, short for Philip. He was cute and nice to me. He was also kind of sexual. At the end of last year, we went out to the park and had sex. Now another guy seems to mean a lot to me. We hold hands in chemistry where we're lab partners and he lets me wear his jacket. But he's also different in a couple of ways. He's very wild, parties a lot, and chews tobacco. Even though I don't drink or run with his crowd, I'd like to date him. Right now, though, my brain and emotional bank feel worn out."

Kate's mother had grown increasingly concerned about her daughter's attraction to blacks. After a few heated discussions, Kate agreed to go into therapy. In this case, the counselor did help Kate piece together her own emotional puzzle.

"I'm adopted," explains Kate. "And because of that, I realized that deep inside I had the feeling that maybe I was partly black. Also, to me, blacks just seem like a much happier people. So in the end, I was specifically seeking out black guys."

In another case, a Russian-born teenager was first involved with a Vietnamese and then a Cambodian. To her perplexed parents, she offered this explanation: she's Asian and they are, too. A fifteen-year-old Puerto Rican girl who only dates blacks says that since she was eight, she's been a Michael Jackson fanatic. Psychotherapist Howells says that the answer is not always as clear as in these situations. The more frequent reason might be that "it's a stage and you're stuck in it. You're stuck in a certain kind of relationship with your parents, so you keep trying to work it through. You keep testing them in the same manner."

Therapist Diamond adds that "you have an obligation to yourself to look at what that's about. Given a random sampling of people, why are you only attracted to someone from a different background? Perhaps you have to look within your own family. What's going on there that seems to make it important for you to see yourself as an outsider? Or to reject the way you've been raised? These answers might tell you that you and your parents should get some help and counseling—together or separately— right away."

RATING YOUR
RELATIONSHIP

The experts we asked suggest that to figure out what's what for an interracial or cross-cultural couple (or for anyone whose relationship with parents is out of kilter), ask yourself this series of questions. If you answer *yes* to ten or more of the following twenty questions, counseling should be a consideration. You should also consider ending the relationship.

YES NO

— — 1. Over the years, have your parents repeated prejudiced comments? ("Lock your doors when you drive down Fourteenth Street." "All those people look alike.")

— — 2. Do you feel like testing their prejudiced feelings?

— — 3. Have you and your parent(s) been fighting a lot lately?

— — 4. Could your dating someone they're against be part of the struggle?

— — 5. Have you been restricted or told you can't use the phone?

— — 6. Have you been forbidden from seeing your partner outside of school?

— — 7. Have you taken your relationship underground?

— — 8. Has the conflict with your parents taken on a life of its own?

— — 9. Is your partner important enough to disrupt your whole world—to cause problems with your family and maybe even to distance you from some friends and relations?

— — 10. Have any of them told you your partner's "bad news"?

— — 11. Have you cut off your friends from your life and found that more often you're just with your partner?

— — 12. Have your grades fallen?

— — 13. Have you been skipping school?

— — 14. Have your eating or sleeping patterns altered?

— — 15. Are you doing a lot of drugs and/or alcohol?

— — 16. Are you having sexual intercourse when you don't really want to?

— — 17. Are you forgetting to practice safe sex?

— — 18. Are you feeling out of control?

— — 19. Are your parents so involved with their own problems that they don't have time for you?

— — 20. Are you being physically, sexually, or verbally abused by a family member, relative, or acquaintance?

Dr. Ponton says, "If your partner has a reputation for getting into trouble, if there's anything involving jail or drug and/or alcohol abuse, if your partner is seeing others besides you, or if your parents and your friends are all against the relationship, I'd be very wary. Look at the whole relationship honestly. When the danger signals add up, they serve as a warning: *Flash, Flash. What you are doing is self-destructive. Get help.*"

For the majority of teens who are part of an interracial or cross-cultural couple, it doesn't have to be part of a pattern. It doesn't have to be a trauma. It can mean that you're attracted to a person who makes you feel good about yourself. You really like one another and you think the same things are important. So what if your backgrounds differ? In fact, those very differences may be part of the attraction.

"You grow up thinking that how you've been raised is the only way," says Diamond. "Then, as you begin to expand your universe, meet other people, maybe travel, you start to see that there are other ways of living. It's very natural to want to learn more about that. It's very natural to decide you've been this one person all your life and now for a while you want to be another—find out about a different race or culture. Some adolescents are genuinely open and are simply interested in a lot of different people. You're color blind."

For some, maybe a white suburban teen, it can be a real identification with the "underdog," as Diamond puts it, a sense of trying to reach out to someone who's a minority, who might be having a hard time. For still others, you could be feeling alienated from your classmates, wanting to make some kind of statement. Howells points out, "Adolescence may be the main time when you have a chance to meet and date different kinds of people. Yes, it's pushing some limits and breaking some unspoken rules. But as long as you're not hurting yourself, or doing anything that you wouldn't do with anybody else, what's the danger?''

LEARNING TO LOVE

Dr. Nolin, sex-educator and sociologist, stresses, "Your first and major task in adolescence is to find out who you are. At this age, you're learning what you're good at and what you're not, how to succeed and how to fail. You're learning that even though your father is determined you'll be an accountant, you could care less. You're deciding what your values are, what is right and wrong and why. And you are setting goals for yourself.

"The other task of adolescence is to develop skills that will enable you to have an intimate relationship. You practice intimacy in your families and in your friendships. Dating and friendships are very important in learning to communicate, to measure your values against others', to give and to get respect and trust. You discover how to go about being a good friend, from providing the shoulder to cry on to understanding it's okay to need comfort, as well.

"Dating and friendships with the opposite sex help you to know yourself and what characteristics you might want in a permanent partner. You begin to see that there are different kinds of love relationships. You can often be very passionately, romantically attached to another teenager. It's more than a friendship, more than just liking the person. You do love that person. But before you really know who *you* are, the kind of love that you're more likely to experience is generally based on trying to fulfill your own needs. You're trying to find acceptance and the excitement of newness. That kind of love is less mature and will often end in time."

There's nothing wrong with being romantically in love and having that relationship end. Part of the teenage experience is that in the process of exploring emotional commitments, you discover wrong turns, dead ends, insurmountable obstacles. And just as true, the more daring the adventure, the more danger along the way. You can't avoid emotional pitfalls; you must learn to get up, walk away, and be wiser.

"Then the time will most probably come when you find somebody who, the more you get to know the person, the more you're able to share who you are," says Dr. Nolin. "You feel more certain that you really do love your partner and that your love will grow. It can turn into true and lasting love, regardless of backgrounds."

7

FAST
FORWARD

We went back at a later time and asked the couples who appeared on these pages the original opening questions: Can you handle the pressure? Is the relationship worth it? Their answers were all over the place. They included "You bet," "Wait-and-see," and "No way." The therapists we consulted said they weren't surprised, pointing to a long laundry list of conditions under which mixed couples have the best chance for success.

Race or ethnic background is far more likely to be an incidental element when the two of you are close in age, have similar interests and pastimes, place the same value on education, come from similar types of homes, hold shared feelings about religion, and have the same sense of your own self-worth. Each step away from a similar world view decreases your chances of being together for very long in the future. This in no way means that dating someone from a different race or culture is bad or wrong. What it does mean, however, is that you face more obstacles when trying to make the relationship work.

Marriage counselors know that, even without the racial or cross-cultural tensions, you've got to factor into the equation all the reasons that any relationship works or falters. How ready you are to be part of a couple. How seriously each of you takes it. How the relationship meshes with your personal priorities and individual values. And in getting to know one another, how much familiarity alters your initial ideal portrait. At that point, do you forget about a possible romance and decide instead that the flawed human isn't worth your affection?

THERESA AND SCOTT

A fast forward on Theresa and Scott from Texas shows this scenario. After the big blowup with his mother, Mrs. Miller, when Scott was sent to stay with relatives, Theresa felt she lived for the ring of the phone. When it finally came, Scott's excuse was he'd been back and forth between his grandmother's and brother's and had been afraid to call. Theresa says, "I agreed to come visit his school in two weeks. Well, I went there and what should happen but Mrs. Miller phoned him and his roommate said, 'Oh, he's out with his girlfriend.' When she got through to Scott, it was the same no-more-money-for-school threat. Then she called me with a repeat of her past curbside performance.

"Where are we now? Nowhere. Scott was always being pulled between me, his family, and school. I can understand the importance of an education, but I kept thinking, Should Scott let his mother run his life the way she does? After all, he is nineteen. And Mrs. Miller is wrong in her feelings toward me, so why should we give up a relationship to prejudice?

"I'm a fighter. I hate to lose both a boyfriend and a best friend in one fell swoop. But I could tell that we were getting all those bad feelings that can collect between two people. Things weren't as much fun anymore. It was always a crisis. When he came back to the Valley for Thanksgiving, I knew something was seriously wrong. As usual, we had to sneak off to see each other. But because I was sure he was going to break up with me, I decided not to let him get the final word.

"We were sitting in his pickup when he said, 'There's something I have to talk to you about.' I said, 'Me, too. I don't think we should see each other anymore.' He looked surprised, then relieved, and within a couple of minutes he was taking me home. Sure, I cried, but thinking back, I'm glad that for once he had a little gumption. He was actually going to tell me good-by face-to-face and not just disappear. But still, who knows what would have happened if by some quirk of fate he'd been born with a different set of parents, say, Mexican-American instead of Anglo.''

KENNY AND MINA

For Kenny and Mina from Southern California, their story came with this ending. After four months of seeing each other, they lost their virginity on his single bed one rainy March afternoon. Mina decided to start marking her menstrual cycle on a calendar so that they could abstain, not have sex, during what she estimated was her most fertile time. They both figured that they were intelligent people; pregnancy was something that only happened to others.

On May thirteenth Mina realized her period was late. For the first few days she thought of excuses. She'd been staying up late to study. To diet, she went twenty-four hours with no food. She was tense. She felt pressure at home, pressure from Kenny. With all that going on, no wonder her system would shut down. So instead of telling anyone, Kenny included, Mina worried alone.

When two weeks had gone by and still no period, Mina let Kenny know her suspicions. "To put it mildly," Mina says, "he was not supportive. In fact, suddenly he's giving me a royal runaround, announcing that his mother has said he can't see me. He said his feelings for me haven't changed, but we have to cool it for a while until he can convince his mom I'm okay. That day was the beginning of the end. Kenny was fine when it was easy and romantic. I think he even kind of got off on the secret part. Our being together was something to throw up at his 'liberal mom.'

"He'd tell me, 'She's a phony. She's backing down on everything she's taught me by giving me a hard time about you.' He thought it was neat when he got her to admit that parents aren't always perfect. Then I overlooked the fact that he was immature; that maybe he saw me as a challenge."

Kenny refused to comment during an attempt at a follow-up interview. Mina had an abortion. At present, she has no desire to date anyone.

IRENE AND RUBEN

The relationship of Irene and Ruben from Ohio took a twist and a turn. After the frightening confrontation with a street gang, the family friend who'd been involved did call Irene's parents. On hearing the news, they decided to seek professional help. "I don't know where the idea came from," says Irene, "but the next thing I knew my super-straight, super-conservative parents had gone to a family health care clinic for advice from a counselor. Then they asked me to go, too, and I agreed. At first I was nervous, because I didn't know what to expect. But the woman I saw explained, 'Let's talk to work out the conflicts.'

"Within a few visits, I began to realize two main things. When I was with Ruben and his friends and his family, I felt they were very loving and open. That was something comforting to me which was missing from my own very restrictive culture. At the same time, I hadn't been able to step back from our relationship and notice how much we both got into the adventure and danger of sneaking around. Now that the counselor suggested to my parents that they let us see each other in the open, some of the excitement has begun to wear off. It's been a month, and even though I still love Ruben, he's not quite as, well, glamorous as he was for me before."

SARA AND BENNIE

An update on Sara and Bennie from New York must be told as both an end and a beginning. After a year and a half during which Sara saw her mother go from disapproving to accepting of the relationship, Bennie graduated from high school. In the fall he went away to college in Pennsylvania to pursue his goal, a career in sports medicine.

"It was a drag in the beginning. We missed each other so much," Bennie says. "During September, we talked almost every day. And then when the phone bills arrived, Sara's mother hit the ceiling. She said writing letters would have to do. But I'm not the best letter writer, and, anyway, I was getting involved in all my new classes, working, meeting new people, and learning my way around. It really is different from high school. I somehow felt older."

Sara offers her perspective. "Not right off, but gradually, I started to get caught up in all that senior stuff. I was still working two nights a week, studying, and I discovered it's perfectly fine not to have a boyfriend. I hadn't really been spending much time just with my girlfriends. Bennie had taken most of my attention. I'd forgotten that girlfriends are important, too. Sure, we still talk about guys, but we talk about where we want to go to college.

"Bennie and I are the first ones in our families to continue on in school. My mother got married when she was real young, sixteen. She had five kids—boom—right in a row. Compared to her, she likes to remind us, we're free as the birds. Then she trots out what we call The Lecture: she wants us to be someone when we grow up. And I don't want to disappoint her and my dad. I know they only want us to have an easier life than they have. Now I feel that Bennie and I will always stay friends. The difference is, though, he's no longer my only future."

KELLY AND RANDALL

Kelly and Randall are feeling upbeat. Recently their relationship made a course adjustment because Kelly's mother happened to run into a former college friend. The two of them got to talking, one topic led to another, and it turned out that the other woman's teenage daughter had a black boyfriend.

She trusted her daughter, she told Kelly's mother. She knew that the teenage years could be tough both on the parent and the child. Her baby was fast becoming an adult. It was hard to let go, but she had to. So what if the kid is black seemed to be her attitude. She, the mother, wasn't going out with him. Her daughter had dated plenty of white creeps, (her word), and this boy didn't appear so bad. As a parent, she decided to remain evenhanded, keep the same rules she'd always had about classes and curfews coming first.

Randall says, "Kelly and I call their meeting a 'happy accident.' Her mother came home and told Kelly about it. She seemed to sort of relax after that." Adds Kelly, "Now Randall can just pop over. He'll stop by and my mother will talk to him. While it's not a real date, it's sure an improvement. And am I ever feeling better! I didn't realize all the pain that I was having by pretending to my parents that Randall didn't matter. I feel like I'm in an open field.

This is so much easier. Now, he's never met my dad and I think that's going to be the next ice-breaking thing. Wish us luck."

JONATHAN AND HEATHER

And what about Jonathan and Heather? Cautious optimism might be the best answer. In lots of ways they are alike—from the comfortable, blended homes they live in to their ice hockey passion and love of Mexican food. There's a healthy competitive edge between them when they compare grades and SAT scores. (Heather's were slightly better.) They're both gregarious, inquisitive, and outgoing by nature. And they both feel it's extremely important to return something to the world around them, not merely to take.

Jonathan says, "To me, it's great having a girlfriend, but it's more than that. She really believes in the relationship. It's a strong bond, a commitment. We always talk about getting married. I also tried to talk her into going to *my* school. Joke, joke. While I'm interested in Brown or Cornell, she wants to go to a smaller school. She knows whatever she chooses will be fine with me.

"Recently I've been thinking a lot about my being biracial. It makes me feel special, like I'm a rare breed. To be one person with the heritage of two cultures is a benefit, not a disadvantage. I have a unique perspective on life. If I'm the worst possible thing that could happen in one of these dating situations, people shouldn't complain. I think I'm terrific. And Heather does, too."

She certainly does. When asked about their future, she admits rather shyly, "Right now I feel like I want to spend the rest of my life with him. And I've never felt that way about anyone else before. The other thing is, I never told a guy that I loved him before Jonathan. But God only knows our future. We're going to colleges at different ends of the world, practically. I don't feel like we're just dating. I don't feel like it's going to end when the summer comes. Right now my plans are aiming for way down the line.

"I don't know how these things work; why you love one person and not another. I never thought about it before. I just went along with everything. I never questioned. I was shocked to find that there was some sort of racism in me, prejudice, whatever you want to call it. It was a blow. It's a bummer, too, to have all these things that put a damper on our relationship that we can't control. I hate not being able to go out on the weekends in my neighborhood, for instance. Then, of course, there's my grandfather."

That's where their story goes full circle. Jonathan's maternal grandparents, who were so crushed when their daughter—his mother—married a black man that they disowned her, are now quite worried. Jonathan's mother says of those days many years ago, "At a time when I needed them, they were not able to be there for me. They didn't know how, because they were so devastated about what my relationship meant to them. Today, though, they're wonderful grandparents to Jonathan. They've far surpassed anything I ever expected. But that's the familiar; that's my son, our family's flesh and blood.

"When Jonathan was first going to Heather's home to meet her parents, it was 'Guess who's coming to dinner?' My parents, Jonathan's grandparents, were very concerned and nervous about that. They said to me, 'Wouldn't it be terrible if Heather's parents didn't accept him?'

"I tried to help them see that isn't it nice that they *are* accepting? But now they've learned about a person their age, Heather's grandfather, whose prejudice locks the door on Jonathan before he can even knock. And my parents cry for this boy, their Jonathan, while their own initial prejudice comes back to haunt them."

QUESTIONS AND ANSWERS

Is interracial and cross-cultural dating on the rise? In the coming years, will this country more accurately reflect its melting pot reputation? Or, in the face of growing racial strife and economic divisions, has dating across cultural barriers actually fallen off? The Justice Department Community Relations Service reports an upward spiral of violence against blacks, as well as against Asian-Americans. A growing perception seems to be that Asians in particular are doing just a little too well financially, and that's sufficient reason to go out and physically attack them.

In addition, some people even predict that by the year 2000, states such as California may well resemble two-tier, unequal societies. At the top will be whites along with well-educated Asians and Asian-Americans holding the professional and technical jobs. On the bottom will be blacks, Latinos, and unskilled Asian-Americans in low-wage and service industry positions. How would that affect who dates whom? Will the lines be more economic than racial or cultural?

The answer is no one really knows for sure. No statistics exist on the past or the future of interracial or cross-cultural dating among adults, let alone teenagers. However, after talking to students from private and public junior and senior high schools around the nation, a kind of consensus was reached: Romance is definitely not going out of style. It's not going to wither. When you look at the potential for dating someone from a background different than your own, most people feel the odds may be high and getting higher. The final opinion is, it's only logical. With increasing numbers of schools integrated, why not students' personal lives, too? The America under eighteen years old is a rainbow of colors.

THE FUTURE AS SEEN
AT I.S. 88

Although a single group can never speak for all students, some ninth graders from I.S. 88, the Peter Rouget Intermediate School in Brooklyn, New York, offered to spend a few hours giving their views on this issue. In fact, they even describe themselves as "the building blocks of the future." When asked about interracial and cross-cultural dating—mixed dating—they laughed. At their school, while most dating may not be interracial, it almost has to cross some geographic bounds. This urban school sandwiched between a highway overpass and a cemetery is what gym teacher Steven Bram dubs "a regular United Nations."

A quick survey of a typical class reveals the following mix. There's Jorge, who was born in Nicaragua and moved here three years ago with his mother, grandmother, and brother. Patricia with her dramatic good looks explains that even though she's from this country, both her parents were born and raised in British Honduras, now known as Belize.

American-born Annie, who's been "seeing" Jorge for the last three weeks, says her roots are Puerto Rican and Spanish. Sharon reports a "hot and cold background." Her father's Italian, while her mother claims Canada as her real home. Kanitia, who's black, replies that she doesn't know exactly where her family comes from. What she does know is that they're all native New Yorkers. And Luisa? "My whole family was born in Colombia and moved to this country when I was about five. I live with my mother, my father, my cousin, and my little brother, age seven."

Bram says, "The school is about fifty percent Hispanic, maybe fifteen percent black, and the rest, thirty-five percent, I guess you'd call 'other.'" That "other" includes not only students primarily of Italian and Irish descent, but also Chinese, Pakistani, Indian, and Arab. "But don't jump to conclusions," adds Luisa. "Even all Hispanics are not alike. The people from each individual country have many different traditions and ways of viewing life." What this translates into at I.S. 88 is that while they all maintain a degree of emotional ties to their home countries, they also learn from each other, creating a "tossed salad culture," Jorge's description. "I'll teach you about my culture; you teach me about yours."

When it comes to dating there is one universal attitude that seems to exist: the double standard. "Girls have regulations, while guys have freedom. I don't think it's fair and I don't think it's right, not women's rights, at least," says Annie. Luisa explains that even her "little brother can go, 'Bye Ma, I'm leaving' and leave," while she has to "sit down and beg her." When Luisa asks, "Why can he do that?" her mother answers, "Because he's a boy; and boys can't get pregnant."

Says Annie, "It's all about protecting our virginity and the possibility of pregnancy. We don't think we should let ourselves be shuffled around like cards. So we try to follow our parents' dating rules which are followed by 'stay home, study to get good grades, and have a career.'"

Another rule for many reads that you aren't allowed to date before your fifteenth, and sometimes sixteenth, birthday. Even for those who can date, there are still various cultural traditions—customs—to follow. Within those boundaries, though, there are enormous variations. Kanitia, for instance, can't go out with anyone, period, until she turns fifteen, a year from now. However, she can and often does spend all evening with "the phone growing out of her ear," as her mother puts it. Kanitia logs in up to three hours a day on the phone.

On the other hand, Patricia went steady nearly all of last year.

Luisa has to deal with a lock on the phone and her father having the only key. In theory, whom she dates is her choice. Reality is different. She explains what happened when a Colombian boy started coming around. "My mother calls him a 'bobo,' a jerk, all because he's Colombian. When he comes to my house, he acts Colombian. What can he do, he is. She says I'd learn more from someone from another culture. In Colombia, the guy goes and meets the girl and talks to the father. I expect him to talk to me, but no. He and my father sit around and watch boxing on TV. That's the Colombian tradition of 'treating a girl with respect.'

"So then when I come home with a Puerto Rican, the guy wants me to go to my bedroom to talk with him. He says that is *his* tradition. Of course my mother says, 'Oh, no, that's not what I mean. If I ever let you see him again, you'll take along your little brother. And, for money, he tells me everything.' 'But Mom,' I say, 'if I hadn't met him, I would never have known that Puerto Ricans make these luscious things called pastellas.' She laughs, then says, 'Watch out. Your father trusts no boy with you.'"

Patricia says her mother "throws fits all the time" because both of Patricia's boyfriends have been of nationalities different from her own. One was Dominican, the other Irish. "My mother says for once she wishes I'd stick to my own kind. With someone with a different background, it always seems to be a problem because they do things differently. They have different habits. So I ask her, 'Where am I going to find a nice British Honduran boy?'"

Luisa interrupts, saying, "That would be booooring. And that's not what this school is about."

Annie calls adults the Maria-and-Tony generation. "They were raised on *West Side Story*, learning stereotypes. We're learning *and* living the facts."

"Right," says Luisa. "When you walk into our lunchroom and see so many different colors, how do you even know for sure who is your own kind? Here, we care more if you're stuck-up or a real lowlife. That's what we're prejudiced against, not background."

No, I.S. 88 is not perfect. There have been times of tension and times of strife. Kanitia mentions the day a mixed couple, black and Latino, were laughed at and called an "oreo cookie." She says, "But that was the worst that happened to them. Adults might have thought, How could those two date each other? We think, What does it matter? It's their business. They're in love. It's a waste to be racist. It's not going to do any good if the races are always at each other. And also, think about all the fun we'd miss without any mixing."

In the end what these students say they'd like to see— for themselves and for others—is that you look at what you share rather than at what you don't. Walk the same streets, shop the same stores, have the same goals, and keep on talking. Then maybe racial and cultural barriers won't keep people apart. They will no longer matter.

At I.S. 88 the students have to take their own advice. They're neighbors. They live next door to each other, some in the nearby small apartment buildings, others in narrow one- and two-family homes. The residents range from welfare recipients to middle class.

Their mothers and fathers are the ones who keep the city running. They are the union member, the security guard, the hairdresser, the electrician, the woman with an office job, the man who owns the deli. Their teenagers want to be the obstetrician, the computer programmer, the psychologist, the economist, the business administrator.

Luisa concludes, "Our parents teach us to learn from the mistakes they made, to do better and play an important role in this country's future. And for us, for all teenagers, that role starts now."

SOURCE
NOTES

CHAPTER 1

1. Howard J. Ehrlich, *The Social Psychology of Prejudice* (New York, 1973), p. 114.

CHAPTER 5

1. "Getting Tough," *Time,* (February 1, 1988), p. 55.

All other quotes are taken
from direct, personal interviews.

APPENDIX

*ORGANIZATIONS THAT ARE
CONCERNED WITH INTERRACIAL AND
CROSS-CULTURAL MATTERS:*

American Field Service International/Intercultural Programs, 313 E. 43rd Street, New York, New York 10017

Association for Multicultural Counseling and Development, 5999 Stevenson Avenue, Alexandria, Virginia 22304 (referrals nationwide)

Biracial Family Network, P.O. Box 489, Chicago, Illinois 60653-0489

Biracial Family Resource Center, 800 Riverside Drive, New York, New York 10032

Breakthrough Foundation, 25 Van Ness, Suite 320, San Francisco, California 94102

The Center for Interracial Counseling, 2265 Westwood Blvd., Suite 151, Los Angeles, California 90064

Council of Interracial Books for Children, 1841 Broadway, New York, New York 10023

Duluth-Superior Interracial Group, 12 E. 4th Street, Duluth, Minnesota 55805

Educational Equity Concepts, Inc., 114 E. 32nd Street, New York, New York 10016

Honoring Our New Ethnic Youth (HONEY), 454 Willamette, #213, Eugene, Oregon 97401

Intercomm, c/o Sharon Sitrin, 202 Garnet Lane, Wallingford, Pennsylvania 19086

INTERace, P.O. Box 7143, Flushing, New York 11354

Interracial Connection, P.O. Box 7055, Norfolk, Virginia 23509

Interracial Families, Inc., 5437 Penn Avenue, Pittsburgh, Pennsylvania 15206

Interracial Families, Inc., Dayspring Christian Center, 700 Second Avenue, Tarentum, Pennsylvania 15084

Interracial Family Alliance, P.O. Box 20280, Atlanta, Georgia 30325

Interracial Family Alliance, P.O. Box 16248, Houston, Texas 77222

Interracial Family Alliance, 194 North Hampton Drive, Willingboro, New Jersey 08046

Interracial Family Circle, P.O. Box 53290, Washington, D.C. 20009

Interracial Family Network, P.O. Box 40466, Portland, Oregon 97240

Interracial Family Unity Network, P.O. Box 6754, Jefferson City, Missouri 65102

I-Pride, 1060 Tennessee Street, San Francisco, California 94107

Multi-racial Americans of Southern California (M.A.S.C.), 12228 Venice Blvd., Suite 425, Los Angeles, California 90066

Multi-racial Families of Central Ohio, c/o 3951 Magnolia Place, Westerville, Ohio 43081

Multi-racial Families of Colorado, P.O. Box 20524, Denver, Colorado 80220-0524

New Race, Inc., P.O. Box 3071, Colorado Springs, Colorado 80934

OURS, Inc., 3307 Highway, North Minneapolis, Minnesota 55422

Parents of Interracial Children, 115 South 46th Street, Omaha, Nebraska 68124

BIBLIOGRAPHY

BOOKS AND BOOKLETS

(Unless otherwise noted, the following titles are Young Adult)

Althen, Gary. *American Ways: A Guide for Foreigners in the United States.* Yarmouth, Maine: Intercultural Press, 1988. (Adult)

Ashabranner, Brent and Paul Conklin, photographer. *The New Americans: Changing Patterns in U.S. Immigration.* New York: Dodd, Mead & Co., Inc. 1983.

Bell, Ruth. *Changing Bodies, Changing Lives: A Book for Teens on Sex and Relationships.* New York: Random House, Inc., 1981.

Eagan, Andrea Boroff. *Why Am I So Miserable if These are the Best Years of my Life?* New York: Avon Books, revised 1988.

Edwards, Gabrielle I. *Coping with Discrimination.* New York: The Rosen Publishing Group, Inc., 1986.

Ehrlich, Howard J. *The Social Psychology of Prejudice.* New York: John Wiley & Sons, Inc., 1973. (Adult)

Gale, Jay. *A Young Man's Guide to Sex.* New York: Holt, Rinehart & Winston, Inc., 1984.

Garver, Susan and Paula McGuire. *Coming to North America: From Mexico, Cuba, and Puerto Rico.* New York: Delacorte Press, 1981.

Hartung, Elizabeth Ann. *Cultural Adjustment Difficulties of Japanese Adolescents Sojourning in the U.S.A.* New York: Research Department of AFS Intercultural Programs, Inc., 1983. (Adult, 22-page booklet)

Huggins, Nathan Irvin. *Black Odyssey: The Afro-American Ordeal in Slavery,* New York: Random House, Inc., 1977.

Lanier, Alison R. *Living in the U.S.A.* Yarmouth, Maine: Intercultural Press, revised 1988. (Adult)

Levy, Marilyn. *Love Is Not Enough.* New York: Fawcett Juniper, 1988.

Madaras, Lynda. *Lynda Madaras' Growing Up Guide for Girls.* New York: Newmarket Press, 1986.

Madaras, Lynda and Area Madaras. *The "What's Happening to My Body?" Book for Girls.* New York: Newmarket Press, 1983.

Madaras, Lynda with Dane Saaveda. *The "What's Happening to My Body?" Book for Boys.* New York: Newmarket Press, 1984.

Meltzer, Milton. *Chinese Americans.* New York: Thomas Y. Crowell Jr. Books, 1980.

————. *Taking Root: Jewish Immigrants in America.* New York: Farrar, Straus, & Co., 1976.

Packer, Alex J. *Bringing Up Your Parents: The Adolescent's Handbook.* Washington, D.C.: Acropolis Books, 1985.

Pedersen, Paul. *Handbook for Developing Multicultural Awareness.* Alexandria, Virginia: American Association for Counseling and Development, 1988. (Adult)

Rohr, Janelle, editor. *The Middle East: Opposing Viewpoints.* St. Paul, Minnesota: Greenhaven Press, 1988.

Smedley, Audrey. *The Origin and Evolution of the Idea of Race.* Boulder, Colorado: Westview Press, 1988. (Adult)

Voss, Jacqueline and Jay Gale. *A Young Woman's Guide to Sex.* New York: Henry Holt & Co., Inc., 1986.

A series of books, each focusing on life in a different part of the world, all published in New York: The Bookwright Press, 1984. *We Live in Australia, We Live in Britain, We Live in China, We Live in Denmark, We Live in France, We Live in India, We Live in Israel, We Live in Italy, We Live in Japan, We Live in New Zealand, We Live in Spain.*

A Fondness for Ice Water: A Brief Introduction to the U.S.A. and Its People. New York: Research Department of AFS Intercultural Programs, 1984. (20 page booklet, also available in Spanish and Thai)

A Selected Annotated Bibliography on the Culture of the U.S.A. New York: Research Department of AFS Intercultural Programs, revised 1987. (Adult, 20 page booklet)

VIDEOS

Cold Water, 40 minutes. Discussion guide. Order from Intercultural Press, P.O. Box 768, Yarmouth, Maine 04096

Mixed Messages: Teens Talk About Sex, Romance, Education and Work. 15 minutes. Discussion guide. Order from Educational Equity Concepts, Inc., 114 E. 32nd Street, New York, New York 10016

INDEX

ABOUT
THE AUTHOR

For more than a dozen years, Janet Bode has worked as a free-lance writer. During this time, she has had four nonfiction books published. *View from Another Closet* and *Fighting Back* were for adults. The other two were both Franklin Watts' young adult publications. *Rape: Preventing It; Coping with the Medical, Legal and Emotional Aftermath* was chosen by the National Council for Social Studies for its award, Outstanding Social Studies Book. *Kids Having Kids: The Unwed Teenage Parent* was cited by the American Library Association in its category Best Books for Young Adults.

Her work also appears regularly in many national periodicals where she covers a wide range of controversial topics from "Love at First Sight" in *Glamour* to "Cocaine Addiction" in *Mademoiselle*. In addition, she collaborates on projects with cartoonist Stan Mack, including an up-coming humorous-mystery-adventure-graphic novel.

Bode has lived and worked not only in the U.S., but also in Europe and Mexico. She now resides in New York City where she is a member of the Authors Guild and the National Writers Union.